THE CITY-ST...

Republican Liberty in a...

Studies in European History

General Editor: Richard Overy
Editorial Consultants: John Breuilly
                       Roy Porter

THE CITY-STATE, 1500–1700

Republican Liberty in an Age of Princely Power

RICHARD MACKENNEY
Lecturer in History
University of Edinburgh

MACMILLAN

First published 1989

Published by
MACMILLAN EDUCATION LTD
Houndmills, Basingstoke, Hampshire RG21 2XS
and London
Companies and representatives
throughout the world

Typeset by Wessex Typesetters
(Division of The Eastern Press Ltd)
Frome, Somerset.

Printed in Hong Kong

British Library Cataloguing in Publication Data
Mackenney, Richard
The city-state, 1500–1700: republican
liberty in an age of princely power.—
(Studies in European history).
1. Europe. City states, 1453–1789
I. Title II. Series
940.2′1
ISBN 0–333–38702–3

Contents

For George Edward
and George Robert Ralph

Editor's Preface

The main purpose of this new series of Macmillan studies is to make available to teacher and student alike developments in a field of history that has become increasingly specialised with the sheer volume of new research and literature now produced. These studies are designed to present the 'state of the debate' on important themes and episodes in European history since the sixteenth century, presented in a clear and critical way by someone who is closely concerned himself with the debate in question.

The studies are not intended to be read as extended bibliographical essays, though each will contain a detailed guide to further reading which will lead students and the general reader quickly to key publications. Each book carries its own interpretation and conclusions, while locating the discussion firmly in the centre of the current issues as historians see them. It is intended that the series will introduce students to historical approaches which are in some cases very new and which, in the normal course of things, would take many years to filter down into the textbooks and school histories. I hope it will demonstrate some of the excitement historians, like scientists, feel as they work away in the vanguard of their subject.

The format of the series conforms closely with that of the companion volumes of studies in economic and social history which has already established a major reputation since its inception in 1968. Both series have an important contribution to make in publicising what it is that historians are doing and in making history more open and accessible. It is vital for history to communicate if it is to survive.

R. J. OVERY

A Note on References

References are cited throughout in brackets according to the numbering in the Bibliography, with page references where necessary indicated by a colon after the bibliography number.

Acknowledgements

In the course of preparing this short work, I have incurred many debts of gratitude. I should record my thanks to Rob Bartlett, whose lucid remarks strongly influenced the conceptual framework. Peter Burke has offered encouragement and advice which were equally welcome. Richard Overy has been as helpful as he has been patient during the over-long process of production, and for their long-suffering courtesy, I thank Vanessa Couchman, Vanessa Graham and Bruce Hunter. Helena Jack worked courageously to produce a typescript. Ian Wei has helped me enormously with the final version. Linda has taken care of George (who would otherwise have proved too engaging a distraction). Without her, the manuscript could never have appeared.

RICHARD MACKENNEY
Edinburgh, 1988

Introduction: Cities and States before 1500

Towns with autonomous political status have been amongst the most dynamic forces in western civilisation. The central concepts in that sentence reveal the enormous influence of the city-state upon the way we think and speak about politics and history, and they show that we cannot define our subject except in terms which the city-state provides. 'Political' derives from the character of life and thought in the city-state of ancient Greece, the *polis*. 'Civilisation' is rooted in the Roman concept of man as a citizen (*civis*) living in a larger community more or less approximating to a city or *civitas* [1–7]. As Aristotle himself said in a phrase often used out of context, 'man is a political animal' or, more accurately, 'man is by nature an animal intended to live in a polis' [*Politics*, I, ii].

Aristotle was describing an entity sovereign within its walls, a face-to-face society, its size limited by the number of people who could hear a summons to a public meeting and who could be reached by the unassisted voice of a single speaker. The polis acknowledged no superior power, and it both assumed and encouraged the involvement of adult male citizens in public life. In that sense, the city-state stood in opposition to the arbitrary rule of a tyrant, and gave life to the idea of freedom [2: ch. 1].

It gave life too to the contradictions of freedom. Does each citizen do as he likes or is his liberty curbed by the will of the majority? And what of the relationship of the insular polis with other communities? Can a city-state remain a city-state if it subjugates a rural area to ensure its own supply of food?

We can apply the abstractions only loosely to the history of the western city-state. Certainly some such entities *did*

1

establish control over rural areas. Federations of city-states sometimes acknowledged the leadership of the greatest member. Some city-states became territorial states and, it might be said, exercised their own tyranny: after all, the Athenian polis and the Roman city-state held sway over colonial empires. Throughout the investigation we should avoid the assumption that we can pin down a typical city state – the very autonomy of the polis demanded and generated a wide variety of historical experience. We should not imagine the oligarchs of Venice or the city-fathers of Amsterdam or the burghers of Eichstätt consulting Aristotle's works to find out what to do next. Instead, we must imagine people acting within the constraints – economic, social, cultural and historical – of their communities and of their times, people seeking to balance their own interests against those of the rest of society and those of other states. Then we perhaps come closer to the historical importance of Aristotle's political theory. For that balancing of interests often involved standing up for the imperfect liberty of a republic against the tyranny – benign or otherwise – of a prince. In that sense, the contradictions of freedom to which Aristotle drew attention remain an integral part of the story.

Athens was gone before the historical questions were answered, the contradictions were unresolved when Rome collapsed, and they remained part of the synthesis constructed in the post-Roman era. With the fall of Rome, the idea of a universal civitas was impossible to apply to this world, and it was transferred to the next. The city-state, the brain-child of the pagan classical world, was one of the chief conceptual and linguistic influences on the greatest work of Christian political thought, St Augustine's *Civitas Dei*, the 'city of God'. Even heaven was conceived to be a city-state [2: p. 815].

The 'dark ages', whose murkiness intensified as Augustine was writing, were centuries without vigorous urban life, but the Christian Church preserved the language of the polis, a language that proved muscular and durable, and which continued to inform the political life of the new type of town which came into being sometime after the year 1000. This new species bred a new type of freedom, for its economy relied on citizens, not slaves. The medieval town saw the rebirth of

2

the civis, the citizen, who shed the status of subject, and relied for his livelihood on his own work, not on unfree labour [8: ch. 8, pt iii].

In medieval Germany, *Stadtluft macht frei* ('Town air makes free') became a legal maxim, and after a year and a day of breathing it, a serf could not be returned to bondage. The town, in short, was the antithesis of the manor, and stood for the supremacy of the law rather than the supremacy of the will, for brotherhood rather than subjection [9: ch. 2, pt ii; 10]. For, paradoxically, the medieval concept of liberty was articulated through brotherhood, through association with other people, a principle elaborated by the towns both within their walls and in their relations with each other. The commune was a sworn association of equals, their mutual dependence a guarantee of their independence of others. As economic life expanded and diversified, as society grew more complicated, the corporations multiplied like healthy cells. Manufacture and market place were regulated by guilds, which also administered charity, and membership of privileged corporations lay at the basis of urban political life [11: chs 4–6]. Economic links with other towns might involve formal diplomatic association in leagues and federations. Their economic importance – and the weakness of alternative forms of state – gave the towns political strength, the strength not merely to survive in a manorial and seigneurial world, but also the strength to defy, to defeat, even to dominate that world. This was the case throughout urban Europe – in the trading network of the Hanseatic towns in the north, in south Germany and Switzerland, and most importantly, all over northern Italy.

In the mid-twelfth century, when the German emperor Frederick Barbarossa (r.1152–90) descended on Italy, his uncle, Bishop Otto of Freising, remarked on the extraordinary liberty, power and social mobility of the Lombard towns, whose impudence his nephew had come to punish. His remarks provide important insights into how a mind accustomed to the feudal world – of those who pray, those who fight and those who work, all of them in rural estates – was stretched and baffled by the society of towns. Let us isolate the most significant of his remarks to make the point:

3

they [the townsmen] are so desirous of liberty that, avoiding the insolence of power, they are governed by the will of consuls rather than rulers . . . as practically that entire land [i.e. Lombardy] is divided among the cities, each of them requires its bishops to live in the cities, and scarcely any noble or great man can be found in all the surrounding territory who does not acknowledge the authority of his city . . . they do not disdain to give the girdle of knighthood or the grades of distinction to young men of inferior station, and even some workers of the vile mechanical arts. (Otto of Freising, *The Deeds of Frederick Barbarossa*, ed. and trans. C. Mierow (New York, 1953) pp. 127–8)

Barbarossa raged and burned and sacked his way through Lombardy in several campaigns, but the towns defeated his feudal host at Legnano (1176), an event still celebrated in northern Italy with cakes shaped like the white doves which were released to signal the victory. The League's rallying cry of 'libertas italica' thereafter became a technical term of diplomatic relations [12: vol. 1, pt 1].

Legnano was the first of many urban triumphs which expressed the vitality of city-states in the deadening world of seigneurial feudalism. In 1204, the Venetians, led by an old, blind doge, Enrico Dandolo, diverted an entire crusading army to destroy first the rival port of Zara and then the capital of the Byzantine Empire: what was stripped from Constantinople became the glory of St Mark's [13: ch. 1; 14: ch. 10].

In northern Europe, the absence of a crusader monarch, Richard I, had led Londoners to declare that their commune would have no king but their mayor [quoted in 15, p. 1]. In the twelfth and thirteenth centuries, a great league of cities, the Hansa, had begun to establish its own networks of diplomacy and defence and its own body of law, making it virtually a federal state [16]. The Hansa's western outpost on the Continent was Bruges, which, with other Flemish towns – Ghent, Liège, Ypres – was a great centre for the production of the cloth which was so essential to the medieval economy. In 1302 the sturdy weavers of Ghent and Bruges stood shoulder to shoulder against the flower of French chivalry at

Courtrai. The townsmen wished the knights 'Good day' with their pikes and halberds (nicknamed *Goedendags*) and amongst the spoils of victory were 700 golden spurs which they hung in triumph in the local church and which later gave their name to the battle itself [17: p. 148].

By then, Italian merchants had created a network of trade which made them masters of the European economy. The war effort of Edward III of England was financed by Florentine banks. When the king reneged on his debts in 1346, the Bardi and Peruzzi companies went bankrupt, sending shockwaves throughout the Continent [18: vol. 2, p. 393].

With the onset of crisis in the late fourteenth century, towns entered a prolonged phase of uncertainty, their dwindling economic power rendering vulnerable their political independence. In Italy, factional struggles resulted in the rise of tyrants at the expense of communal liberty. Indeed by 1400 it seemed that the whole peninsula might succumb to the rule of Giangaleazzo Visconti, Lord of Milan. But the Florentine Republic resisted him, and in doing so its citizens found a new confidence in their cultural capacities. We need not assert that Florentine republicanism *caused* the Florentine Renaissance, but we need to acknowledge that the unusually close relationship of republican politics and civic culture imparted to the Renaissance one of its most fundamental and original features [19;20]. Jakob Burckhardt was pointing to this connection of politics and culture when he elaborated his famous concept 'the State as a Work of Art' [21]. As a physical environment, the city-state of Florence was precisely that. In material terms, the Renaissance meant the embellishment of the urban fabric. The cathedral of Florence was a civic project, it was the guilds of the city who sponsored statues for the 24 public niches at Orsanmichele [22]. Of course, Florence was no democracy, its politics were strictly oligarchic, but there is something exhilarating about the celebration of the creative layman as the citizen of a free republic, and we should remember Renaissance Florence for its aspirations as well as for its shortcomings [23; 24; 25].

As a republic, Florence was not typical of Italian states, still less of Europe as a whole. It became so when, under the Medici, it gradually succumbed to princely rule. This brings us to our subject – or non-subject:

For how can we think of the Middle Ages without thinking of the cities, and yet who thinks of them after 1500? [26: p. 57]

Few essays have proved as controversial as Hugh Trevor-Roper's brilliant piece, 'The general crisis of the seventeenth century' [27; 28]. Yet his comments on the demise of cities, which drew attention to how little had been written on the subject, have brought few rejoinders and excited scant debate. The question he posed – a question fundamental to the nature of how modern Europe developed – remains unsolved. What follows is an attempt to suggest some lines of inquiry which may help to make sense of this complicated problem. There are bound to be oversimplifications and distortions, there are no doubt a number of lacunae, yet some sort of synthesis is long overdue. For historians may read as much as they choose about the city-state before 1500: about the classical polis, the medieval commune, the Renaissance republic. There is even a vast literature on early modern cities as economic entities [18]. But there is little to be found on the subject of the early modern city-state beyond what Braudel wrote many years ago [29: vol. 1, pp. 338–54] – which inspired Trevor-Roper's comments in the first place.

The history of the early modern city is therefore paradoxical. After 1500, towns became much more obvious in the economic and social life of Europe. In 1500 there were some 26 towns with a population of 40,000 or more. By 1600 there may have been as many as 42 in this category [30: pp. 42–3]. The great booming economy of the sixteenth century is incomprehensible without the continuing prosperity of Venice, of Augsburg and Genoa, the sudden wealth of Lyons, Antwerp and Seville. Yet as political centres we think not of these but of Brussels, Madrid, Paris or London, the capital cities of territorial monarchies.

In an imaginary scene in his *Advertisements from Parnassus*, (1612), Traiano Boccalini made an early attempt to quantify the decline. Lorenzo de' Medici is given a balance in which to weigh the powers of Europe: expanding France shows 25 measures; the global power of Spain 20; Venice, the largest of the city-states, a mere 8 [116].

6

This essay covers a period of apparently unrelieved decay in the fortunes of politically autonomous cities. In 1499, the French ambassador in Venice, Philippe de Commynes, recorded his impressions of the political destiny of what he described as 'the most triumphant city':

> I tell you that I found them so knowledgeable and so intent upon expanding their Lordship, that if provision is not soon made, all their neighbours will curse the time ... I say once more that they are on the road to future greatness. (translated from *Mémoires*, ed. J. Calmette, 3 vols (Paris, 1925) vol. 3, ch. 18, pp. 113–14)

What monarch feared a city-state in 1700? By then Louis XIII had long since crushed the liberties of La Rochelle, the Great Elector had humbled Königsberg. And in the affairs of Europe as a whole, the city-state of Venice, even though it preserved its independence, could not compete with the resources of the territorial monarchies. Princes had long been jealous of the autonomy of towns, and had long coveted their wealth. In the sixteenth and seventeenth centuries, princes at last possessed the means with which to realise their ambitions.

The fate of great cities seems universally the same, and Trevor-Roper's thesis looks incontestable. Whatever their economic might, their political fortunes were never in their own hands. Seville was sucked of its American treasure by the wars of Castile, the fortunes of Lyons were dictated by civil war in France as a whole, Antwerp's money bags were easily opened by Spanish swords.

The early modern period, then, apparently witnesses the demise of the autonomous city and its style of politics, for with the city-state went republicanism and federal experiment. All were crushed by the weight of princely absolutism, that exotic phenomenon which pointed imperiously toward the modern sovereign state.

There is no doubt that the cities, expanding economically, were squeezed politically. But they were not all equally malleable and the squeeze did not produce uniform or necessarily predictable results. As Brian Pullan has demonstrated, the relationship between towns and states – even at the end

7

of the sixteenth century – was delicate and complicated, and we must not oversimplify the pattern of either's destiny [31]. The rest of this essay suggests that the consolidation of territorial states often involved the military defeat of urban liberties (chapter 1), that the process of subordination was followed and reinforced by the growth of capital cities – with all their social problems – and of national markets (chapter 2). The climax of the argument (chapter 3) is a tangled and neglected story of the survival and continued vigour of autonomous towns, of federations, of republicanism – and of their influence upon the liberties of the modern West, liberties identified with a 'free world', a vast and complex world which has yet to resolve the contradictions of the tiny polis of the ancient Greeks.

1 Defeat

The materials with which cities were built remained fundamentally unchanged from the time of Pericles to the Industrial Revolution [1]. What could destroy them changed drastically in the sixteenth and seventeenth centuries. That period witnessed a massive increase in the scale, duration and cost of warfare which was a decisive influence on the character of the absolutist state [32–36]. It is important to remind ourselves of what these developments were, at least in outline. It is ironic, but already a testimony to the complexity of our subject, that we should begin with the defeat of a princely army. In 1477, mounted Burgundian knights were routed by the pikes of Swiss footsoldiers. This was not the first defeat of horsemen by infantry – we need only remind ourselves of Morgarten, Courtrai and Agincourt – but this time the victory proved something of a turning point. Mercenaries became the Swiss Confederation's most sought-after export ('no money, no Swiss' is a phrase which dates from this era) and this was part of a fundamental change in the size and balance of European armies. The expensive, armour-clad horseman gave place to the pikeman, and large armies of commoners replaced armed bands of nobles. In 1470, the armies of the Spanish monarchy numbered some 20,000, in 1550, 150,000, in 1600, about 200,000, by which time the battle-hardened *tercios* were the finest soldiers in Europe. The army of France was some 40,000 strong in 1475, by 1595 it had doubled. There were 150,000 soldiers in the armies of Louis XIII in the 1630s and Louis XIV could boast of a staggering 400,000 men under arms in 1705 [33: ch. 4]. Increasing numbers of soldiers were armed with firearms (and it was easier to train someone to shoot a gun than a bow [35: pp. 151–2]) which made for more destructive war. The greater complexity of tactics which involved pikemen, arquebusiers, swordsmen and artillery made it important for the soldier to acquire the discipline of a professional. He was engaged in longer campaigns, too, for advances in the technology of firearms were countered, even outpaced, by improvements in fortification. From the fifteenth century onwards, strongholds from Berwick to Malta and from Danzig to La Rochelle were protected with lower, thicker walls, elaborately spiked with bastions less vulnerable than before to cannon or to frontal assault [32]. The vast commitment of human and material resources to the waging of war among states had a grim and relentless impact on towns. Independent cities could not mobilise such forces, or pay for such walls. Cities whose wealth depended on the careful calculations of merchants were prey to spendthrift princes who devoted their budgets to war and mortgaged their economies to raise armies which would consolidate princely power at home and abroad.

The proud towns of Flanders were crushed by the dukes of Burgundy [17; 37]. In 1452, as so often before, Ghent was in rebellion. This time its defences were battered by siege guns, and on the field of Gavère the following year the civic militia was overpowered by the veterans of the ducal army. Philip the Good imposed an indemnity of 350,000 gold ridders and forced the city to renounce its independence. He was positively soft compared with his successor. Charles the Rash exacted tribute from Ghent and Michelin, and engaged in an aggressive and expansionist war against Liège (not even a Burgundian town) which he sacked and put to the torch in 1468.

Charles's defeat and death at the hands of the Swiss in 1477 led to the collapse of Burgundian power, but there was no urban recovery. The cities' anachronistic attempts to restore the democracy which they had possessed in the Middle Ages resulted in violent anarchy and capitulation to the Emperor Maximilian, heir to the Burgundian lands, in 1494. The last outcry of the guilds of Ghent in 1539 led to confrontation with a duke who happened in addition to be ruler of half the known world. Charles V took an army 5000 strong to Ghent, used his cannon against the city, executed thirty 'ringleaders', confiscated property, humiliated the townsfolk and imposed a fine in keeping with his stature as a monarch. He abolished any remaining autonomy by removing the constitution and appropriating the right to nominate the alderman. He even put an end to the physical separateness of the city by filling in the moat [17: pp. 216–19].

A similar process was under way in Brandenburg [38]. A succession of margraves cut the towns of the region away from the Hanseatic League. In 1440, Berlin and Cölln lost all their privileges, their independence, and their union with other towns. The fortress subsequently built at Cölln was a symbol of princely triumph and was described in the chronicles as 'a rein on ancient liberty'. In the 1470s and 1480s the towns protested against princely exaction, most specifically against a tax on beer. In 1488 the town of Stendal was in revolt, but an intimidating show of force set the burghers on their knees in homage, and cutting off some heads induced the city's agreement to a doubling of the tax. This was followed by the pacification of Osterburg and Salzwedel, of Seehausen, Weben and Gardelegen until,

> at the close of the Middle Ages, the political power of the Brandenburg towns was completely broken, the craft guilds and commons were subservient to the patricians, and the latter depended on the margarve. [38]

As in Ghent, urban magistrates became princely nominees, and urban self-government went into leprous, unrecognisable decay – even the Reformation could not revive it.

By 1500, population increase had begun to cheapen the price of labour, reversing conditions which had prevailed since the Black Death. At the same time, the shrill paeans of tame humanists urged princes to imitate the ancients by enforcing Roman law – a code which acknowledged only private and public property, and which remorselessly gobbled up common land, turning Germany into a mosaic of petty absolutisms [39]. From their stable power bases in the countryside, the princes turned greedily to the towns. The cities lacked the strength to stand against them. Cologne could not confront the electors of Mainz and Trier as well as its own archbishop – politically and economically, it could not afford the Reformation [40]. Mainz and Erfurt lost their independence per-

11

manently, Worms and Regensburg for a while. The Wittelsbachs coveted Regensburg, and Augsburg too, the Franconian Hohenzollerns strove to bring Nuremberg to heel [41]. There was other business at the Diet of Worms in 1521, but at the time, Luther's protest was less striking than the new aggressiveness which the princes displayed towards the cities, especially through a new governing council headed by the Count Palatine Frederick [41: p. 120].

The princes were not the only threat. The Emperor Maximilian mortgaged cities to the princes or bled them white for himself. At his death in 1519, apart from the 1.3 million he owed the Fuggers, some 100,000 florins were still due to the cities of Augsburg, Strasbourg, Nuremberg, Basel and Freibourg im Breisgau [41: p. 82]. To his successor, Charles V, the extirpation of heresy was far more important than the support of the towns for his empire, and he was quite prepared to destroy not just Lutheranism but also its urban seed-bed. After the Emperor's triumph over the Protestants at Mühlberg (1547), his forces occupied Wittenberg (even Charles was surprised that Luther's town did not put up a fight), Tecklenburg, Osnabrück, Hoya, Schaumburg and Minden [42: bk. III, ch. 3]. Between 1548 and 1552, he abolished the constitutions of 28 'free' cities [43]. Zwingli's prediction that 'under the guise of religion, the free cities will lose their liberties' seemed to be coming true [41: p. 203]. When the emperor himself was ignominiously humbled by the League of Torgau, the government of Germany became a matter for the princes. After the Peace of Augsburg (1555), it was the prince's wish that determined whether a particular territory would be Catholic or Lutheran [44: pp. 243–6].

The Augsburg settlement at least opened a half-century of relative peace in Germany. Then the Thirty Years War broke out. As the vast armies of Wallenstein and Gustavus Adolphus careered around with unprecedented ferocity, many cities could only resign themselves to destruction or bankruptcy, or both. Nuremberg bought off successive assailants, the municipal debt growing from 1.8 million gulden in 1618 to 7.4 million at the end of the war. That was better than the sack which often followed defiance. In 1631, as the Swedes destroyed Kustrin and Frankfurt-on-Oder, their ally Magdeburg fell to the imperialists, and 20,000 inhabitants were put to the sword [45].

The age of religious war saw the end of urban liberties in France, too. Paris had excluded Henry III in 1588, but six years later it was tamed by his successor after a siege. 'Never again did the ideology of lost liberties serve effectively to rally the Parisians against the Crown' [46: p. 51]. Military conquest was followed by increased policing, high-handed censorship, and the manipulation of elections. Henry IV's Paris foreshadowed the docile capital of Louis XIV.

Far to the west stood La Rochelle, the Protestant 'state-within-a-state'. This 'effectively autonomous political community' was brought to heel by a royal army in 1628 [47: p. 4]. If we choose not to describe this coastal town as a city-state, we fight the opinion of the king who sought to subdue it. He attacked the citizens' freedom of association (see above, p. 7]. He wanted an end to Protestant synods, which he defined as:

> illicit assemblies which were better employed in popular and republican states than to maintain the obedience which is naturally due to us. [quoted in 47: p. 33]

In the year or so of siege, between death and departure, La Rochelle lost some 15,000 inhabitants – about 60 per cent of its population.

The histories of Germany and France in the sixteenth and early seventeenth centuries are dominated by religious conflicts. We should remember, however, that the assertion of princely power in Burgundy and Brandenburg preceded the Reformation. The process we are examining is first and foremost the triumph of the secular state. The point is made by reference to Catholic countries which were not torn apart by religious wars, but where a similar pattern of princely domination unfolded.

It was in Italy, after all, that the design of the bastion developed; it was in Italy that the princes of France and Spain gained their first triumphs; in Italy that the beginnings of changes in the style of war were marked by spectacular bouts of destruction. In 1494 Charles VIII's invading army consisted of 9000 cavalry and 9000 infantry. In 1525 Francis I had an army of 30,000 in the field, but only 6000 were mounted. One reason for the new emphasis on infantry was the triumph of the Swiss. In 1509, their alliance with France lapsed. The mercenary armies of Matthias Schinner, cardinal bishop of Sion, expelled the French from Milan in the same year and routed a French campaign of 1513. What spelled doom for the Swiss pikemen was the raking gunfire of artillery and arquebuses which made new and devastating contributions at Cerignola (1503), Ravenna (1512), Marignano (1515), Bicocca (1522) and Pavia (1525) [48].

Meanwhile, the Italian city-states collapsed as though the Renaissance had been so much brittle tinsel. According to Machiavelli, Charles VIII conquered Italy in 1494 with weapons no more formidable than the sticks of chalk used by his billeting officers to mark houses for his troops. Piero de' Medici gave away Florence's Tuscan fortresses and Charles entered the city as conqueror. After the disaster of Agnadello (1509), the Venetians returned to the lagoon to lick their wounds and thereafter relied for their recovery on the divisions of their enemies, not their own strengths [48]. As the wars dragged on, Siena was humbled by the cost of new fortifications – a classic instance of the demise of a city-state. Its small labour force, the problems of drumming up soldiers and supplies, its responsibilities for other, smaller towns – all this compounded the problem of paying for the new walls demanded by the emperor, whose intention was to control civic disagreement through a military presence. The Sienese were threated by the fortress both as a military installation and as a financial burden, and revolted against Habsburg control. However, the expulsion of the Spaniards merely flung the Sienese into dependence upon a French alliance, and when that failed, the city was forced to surrender on the emperor's terms:

Refortifying her state bankrupted Siena and left her without resources to raise the field armies she needed for her defences, to hire and man the galleys to relieve her vital coastal ports, or to supply her beleaguered garrisons. The military revolution of the sixteenth century had eventually

14

determined the destruction of one of the last great medieval Italian communes. [49]

The Spanish soliders so prominent in the Italian wars were also required to quell urban liberties at home. In Castile in 1521, the autonomous cities, the *comunidades* – Burgos, Medina, Toledo, Valladolid – were in open revolt, close to revolution. But the citizen armies were bloodily defeated by the armies of the Crown at Vilalar and again outside the walls of Valencia. That was the last revolt against the monarchy in Castile [50].

Since the domestic affairs of Spain are so often neglected by historians, it is ironic that the character of the 1521 rebellion should have raised controversial questions concerning the struggles of towns and princes in Europe as a whole. Does the historian describe the progressive republicanism of the towns crushed by the conservative forces of royal absolutism? Or does he discuss the outdated privileges of medieval cities overriden by a new, dynamic force, namely the territorial state [51: pp. 254–74]?

Neither juxtaposition – progressive *versus* conservative, medieval *versus* modern – is particularly satisfactory, not least because the terms would have been incomprehensible to both townsmen and princes. The point to be made is this: both cities and states were dynamic forces in the early modern world, but it became increasingly clear that the co-existence of rival sovereignties could not be peaceful. Ghent, Osnabrück, La Rochelle, Burgos, Siena, all had to be subordinated militarily and politically if the central state was to overcome the problem of regional diversity. Autonomous cities could either attempt to centralise a power of their own, or succumb to the central power of the prince. They could eat or else be eaten. In the age of the 'military revolution', the latter was always more likely.

Military conquest – dazzling as its history may be – should not obscure a slower process which was also under way. The subordination of the cities by armed force was followed and underpinned by new economic, social and political constraints.

2 Integration

The emergence of princely states did not mean that towns ceased to figure in the political calculations of state-builders. The central sovereign power was 'the conqueror of towns, but heir to their institutions and ways of thinking and completely incapable of dispensing with them' [18: vol. 1, p. 514]. The enemies were dependent on each other, and in the course of the sixteenth and seventeenth centuries, the victorious state recast the vanquished city in its own all-conquering image.

Reasons of state began to dictate changes in the physical appearance of towns. The state's military impact meant drastic architectural alteration. By the seventeenth century, space had to be left or created for parade grounds and barracks. Urban design laid greater emphasis on wide avenues which gave troops freedom of movement. Sometimes broad boulevards were conceived as converging at a central point commanded by cannon. Thus the state 'drives headlong into the city centre . . . which symbolised the collection of public power in a centralised institution or a despotic prince' [1: p. 349]. The absolutist state became an overtly military institution, but between the prince at the centre of the state and the army at its perimeter stood the court, a vast and expanding body of aristocrats and bureaucrats, courtiers and officials, advisers and toadies, all of them creating affairs of state as they dealt with them [52].

It was the court that dictated the patterns of social life in Europe's major cities. Some cities – most obviously Paris and Madrid – had no special commercial importance without the court. These were centres where the demands of the state's servants – great aristocrats or aspiring bourgeois – for food, clothes, carriages and domestics, determined the economic profile of the city, especially as the peacocks who surrounded

17

the prince sought to outdo each other in the lavishness of their plumage [1: ch. 12; 53: ch. 10].

Not all courts were centred in capital cities (one thinks of Naples, Milan and Palermo), but nearly all capitals (Venice is an exception) had courts, and the social and economic pressure of the court was at its greatest when the city which hosted it was also the home of an absolute monarch.

In the sixteenth century, Florentine republicanism was not merely laid to rest, it was buried under the magnificence of the Medici, hereditary rulers of Tuscany under the constitution of 1532, and eventually Grand Dukes of Tuscany. What could be further from the austere drama of Masaccio's 'Tribute Money' (c. 1425), with its message about things higher than Caesar, than Vasari's gaudy celebration of the apotheosis of Cosimo I in which God and Caesar become one? Cosimo dominates the ceiling of the Palazzo Vecchio like the sun – especially since the planets are shown in orbit around him. Could Donatello have spoken of old Cosimo's children in the fifteenth century as Bronzino spoke of Duke Cosimo's a century later, 'Our angels are all very well and are adored' [quoted in 54: p. 105]? The cult of the prince, the expansion of the court and the growth of bureaucracy went hand in perfumed glove. The vast buildings which presently house Florence's principal art gallery, the Uffizi (designed, like the 'Apotheosis', by Vasari) were originally precisely that, 'Offices' to house the servants of the state [3: p. 121].

The pattern is repeated as far away as Vienna. The court of Ferdinand II *was* the Habsburg state, so how could a state capital exist without the court [52: ch. 6]? Madrid and Paris were even grander theatres of monarchy and provide valuable histories of how the princely court shaped the character of urban life.

The creation of a capital at Madrid was 'a triumph of policy over plausibility' [55: p. 1]. No one knows quite why the court transferred there in 1561 – abandoning Toledo and disdaining Valladolid – yet the court's presence created the capital, and the prince had to house his court. Philip II spent 5.25 million ducats on his retreat, the Escorial, which was built between 1563 and 1584. In the 1630s, Philip IV's Buen Retiro cost some 3 million ducats a year to construct, about 10 per cent

18

of the royal budget. That huge figure does not include salaries or entertainments – masques, plays, pageants, dances, banquets, visits to the royal zoo – for some 1700 members of the household and 400 councillors and officials. In 1675, it was reckoned that a month at the Retiro cost about 80,000 ducats, rather cheaper than 20 days at the Escorial, which cost 120,000.

The interiors of such palaces were appropriately opulent. Philip IV (1621–65) added about 2000 paintings to the royal collections. The rest of the furnishings included luxuries so elaborate that they too might be regarded as works of art. Some of the tapestries hung to make the chambers warmer cost as much as 6000 ducats, the royal bed 2500, a single cabinet 30,000, a table service 10,000 . . . and so on. What the court spent, or promised to spend, on splendid clothes and other luxuries is impossible to calculate with precision, but the nine hundred carriages which rolled through the streets of Madrid in 1637 suggest the scale of 'conspicuous consumption' [52: ch. 8; 53: ch. 10; 55].

The sumptuous pattern of material life was similar in seventeenth-century Paris, a city remodelled by Henry IV, by Richelieu and by Louis XIV. The new buildings were necessary to house government officals – whose numbers doubled in Paris in this period. After his pacification of the city, and in some ways as part of it, Henry IV impressed on Parisians the greatness of the monarchy with monuments such as the new Louvre and the galleries added to the Tuileries. He stamped imperial classicism on the Place Royale and Place Dauphine and on the Hôpital Saint-Louis. From 1631, under Richelieu's guidance, the Palais Royal became 'a veritable ministerial quarter, the political and courtly centre of France'. The subordination of the city to the state was demonstrated by the way an official's rise to power could be charted by his shifts of residence: from Saint Louis to Saint Germain, from Saint Germain to the 'Quartier Richelieu', as the Palais Royal came to be known [46: p. 93].

As in the case of Madrid, the economic pressure of courtly demand appears inconceivable considering that mass production of the essentials of everyday life was unknown. Luxury entered every detail of political life, even under the hard-bitten state-builder Cardinal Richelieu. His *Political Testament* included the recommendation that chambers in which the king conducted business should be freshened with perfume five or six times a day. As a collector, his successor Mazarin rivalled Philip IV, owning 500 paintings in 1652, then acquiring more, constantly embellishing his surroundings with an endless array of bronzes, medals, jewels, furniture, crystal vases, books, clocks, ivories, precious cloth [46: p. 253].

The splendours of palace life glowed all the more brightly when touched by the rays of the Sun King. In 1665, Christopher Wren observed of the old château of Versailles that its recent refurbishment had left 'not an inch within but is crowded with little curiosities of ornaments' [quoted in 56: p. 40]. That was before Versailles was converted into a vast complex of buildings which made Paris unnecessary to the king's itineraries – he hardly ever visited the city, for Versailles was a city in itself. There were special residences for royal dogs and royal bastards, and for 12,000 royal horses. (There was room too for a garrison of 14,000 to remind the subject that divine right also had its earthly sanction.)

Again there was huge pressure on the mechanisms of production for both interior and exterior. Mirrors had to be supplied for the famous gallery 75 metres long. And a whole industry, the Gobelins tapestry works, was established to furnish the royal household with elegant insulation. Versailles became a vast showroom, and its development and replenishment were second only to military glory in the king's priorities. Between 1644 and 1690, 80 million *livres* were spent on the palace. The figure for 1685 alone was 11 million, including more than 600,000 spent on a new orangery. Most of that was for shifting earth for the 2000 orange trees which were later imported from Italy. The two main projects for supplying water cost a total of 13 million *livres*. About 1.7 million was spent on paintings, 2.7 million on sculpture – one single parterrre required the commissioning in 1674 of 28 marble figures, all larger than life.

Lists of this sort may not convey the extravagant elegance of court life, but they prompt reflection on the scale and sophistication of the economic structures required to meet such demand. The princely court was a huge market for high-quality goods produced by skilled craftsmen and artists, and in this way, many urban economies were geared to the aristocratic tastes of princes and courtiers. Where, for instance, was the incentive for guilds to change their traditional mechanisms of production in such circumstances? Silk weavers as far away as Lyons or Nîmes were heavily dependent on the court as a market for their gorgeous wares [57].

In this curious way, the capital, a market for life's inessentials, helped forge a national market. This in turn meant that life's necessities had to be produced elsewhere. While urban guilds pandered to the tastes of the court for refined luxuries, manufacturers took industry to rural areas. In this way they by-passed the guild system (which was geared to high-quality and high-cost production) and gave work to an unorganised labour force in the countryside eager to supplement thin incomes with domestic work [18: vol. 2, ch. 3].

The traffic of enterprise and endeavour was two-way. The expansion of cities before the Industrial Revolution depended on immigration from the countryside, and it was the constant stream of immigrants which offset the high death rate of the urban population [18: vol. 1; 58]. In the seventeenth century, when the population of Europe grew only sluggishly, European capitals continued to swell, sometimes at the expense of other centres. In 1546, fifteen years before the court arrived, the population of Madrid was about 30,000. In 1630 it may have been as high as 180,000. Toledo, the traditional capital of Castile, had a population of 60,000 in 1571, but this had shrunk to 25,000 by 1646. Between 1570 and 1600, Madrid doubled its population and therefore its consumption. How is this to be explained? Between 1563 and 1597, Madrid absorbed some 1400 immigrants a year. Between 1597 and 1630 the rate increased to something like 4600. Toledo was losing 1500 people a year at this time, a process accelerated by the frequent appropriation of regional food resources by Madrid, whatever the needs of other cities [59].

Immigration on a similar scale was under way in London, which attracted about 5500 outsiders a year around 1600, preparing for its role as the commerical powerhouse of a world empire [18; 60]. And one must remember that here too there was a court, and conspicuous consumption generated by the

21

London 'season' with its calls for luxuries and servants [18: vol. 1].

In Madrid, Paris and London, the expansion of metropolitan society produced its own stresses and strains. A large proportion of the new population was, in social and economic terms, unstable. Madrid had its picaresque underworld. The number of beggars in Paris quadrupled in the course of the seventeenth century [61]. In London, Bridewell prison held 69 vagrants in 1560, more than 500 at the end of the century. Not all of them arrived as vagrants, but many became so as their future evaporated [60]. The workforce was vulnerable to under-employment: apprentices and wage labourers lacked security and prospects. This group, mainly young males lacking steady work, was less likely to be able to establish a settled family life, which in turn made it more susceptible to natural decrease. The gaps were filled by more immigrants, which compounded the problem by creating a larger unstable population [58].

The traditional economic and social structures of urban Europe could not cope with the expansion of the sixteenth century and the continued growth of capital cities in the seventeenth. Perhaps the most obvious symptom of the malaise was poverty, as conspicuous as the profligate extravagance of the courtly elite [53].

In the early modern period, the relief of poverty increasingly became a 'national' problem, the responsibility of central government or of the supra-national machinery of the Counter-Reformation. The traditional agencies of poor relief in the towns, guilds and confraternities, with their concern for the well-being of a strictly defined membership, were not equipped to deal with indigence on a large scale in society as a whole. Even Toledo, with its declining population, tended to seek help from external sources [62]. In seventeenth-century Madrid, the clergy distributed some 30,000 bowls of soup every day. In Paris, beggars were confined for their spiritual well-being to the Hôpital General [61]. The capital became a base from which St Vincent de Paul sought to attack rural poverty through what has been described as a 'national philanthropy' [63]. In England too, the authorities set about the relief of a national problem, and their initiatives may have checked the worst effects of dearth at crucial moments such as the gruesome 1590s [64; 65].

22

Even the brief surveys contained in this chapter and the last give the clear impression that the early modern period witnessed the steady demise of the city-state. Autonomous towns were incorporated, often harshly, into grander political entities, and there was an economic imperative which drove the cities into a broader and more complicated pattern of demand. This was the case even in that ramshackle miscellany of autonomies, the empire. T. A. Brady succinctly explains why, in the final analysis, more German towns did not join the Swiss Confederation:

> Purely local action could never relieve the Augsburg cannon-founder of his need for Tyrolean copper, the Nuremberg merchant's worry about his goods in transit from Lyons, the Strasbourg butcher's concern to buy Hessian sheep and Hungarian cattle, or the Ulm fustian weaver's demand for Egyptian cotton. [41: p. 228]

We can pull together the arguments of the first two chapters with the idea of scale. Neither Aristotle's face-to-face community, nor the self-contained vigour of the medieval commune could survive in a world in which the traditional patterns of economic, social and political life were dislocated and swollen out of recognition. The cities could not match the armies of the prince, they could not detach their economies from the demands of the prince and the aristocracy, they could not cope with increasing social problems associated with sprawling capital cities and burgeoning national markets.

After 1500, life grew too complicated, it seems, to be contained within the sovereign girdle of a city wall. Such at least is the general pattern in Spain, France and Britain, as viewed from Madrid, Paris and London. Though Germany never found a permanent capital in our period, the emergence of Brandenburg with its centre fixed and stable at Berlin seems to presage the dominance of Prussia in the nineteenth century. By contrast, the survival of smaller states in divided Italy might be interpreted as ensuring the decline of the peninsula in the affairs of Europe.

There is nevertheless a danger in overstating both the inevitability and the completeness of the national state's emergence. It is all too easy to ignore the continuation of the politics, the society, the culture, yes, and the independence of cities, republics and federations which did not fall in with the triumphal progress of absolute monarchs and central states.

24

3 Survival

From the standpoint of an industrial Europe, a Europe whose most powerful legacy to the world it once dominated is nationalism, it is easy to rationalise the emergence of the modern state. A series of experiments – feudal monarchy, new monarchy, absolute monarchy – were given modern form by the change in the balance of social forces which underpinned the state in France in 1789. The bourgeoisie – lawyers and professional men – overturned the sovereignty of the monarch and in its stead constructed a representative assembly which embodied the sovereignty of the nation. This decisive shift was confirmed throughout Europe in the nineteenth century by the economic triumph of the middle classes in the Industrial Revolution [66; 67].

This chapter offers a reminder that the consolidation of sovereign central power was only one aspect of state development in early modern Europe: there was plenty of room for a wide variety of forms, often within the bosom of absolutist states, and we must be careful not to read back the nation-states of the nineteenth century into earlier periods, not least because of the weakness of national consciousness before the French Revolution [68]. Indeed, the most vital political nuclei of the sixteenth and seventeenth centuries were still the towns, for many of them fought off princely armies and retained their economic independence. Sometimes – as in Germany – the cities survived as city-states, sometimes they formed federations, as in the case of the Swiss. Sometimes the oligarchs developed their own collective absolutism – as has been argued in the case of Venice and Amsterdam [69; 70]. The point to make before we study the particulars of each area, is that the three processes which this work highlights – defeat, integration, survival – were not distinct or mutually exclusive. They co-existed and overlapped, they involved a complicated interpenetration of values as well as straightforward conflict. Each of the three historical experiences has its own complexity, its own contradictions, as closer examination reveals.

The Spanish Monarchy

The process of conquest, we should remember, was fraught with uncertainty as far as the princes were concerned. Some of the most spectacular instances of urban destruction were symptoms of a breakdown in the machinery of state, not of its smooth efficiency. The German mercenaries who sacked Rome in 1527, and the soldiers who unleashed the 'Spanish Fury' on Antwerp half a century later were on the rampage because they had not been paid.

As for rebellion, the outcome was not always clear at the outset. The *comunidades* of 1521 nearly succeeded in changing the political shape of Castile. The regent's flat panic when faced with rebellion was followed by humiliation when the citizens of Medina del Campo denied him access to his precious artillery. Then the rebels missed their chance by failing to negotiate when they held the upper hand. Even so, as if to defy the new developments in the conduct of war, the Crown's victory at Vilalar was decided by the superiority of royal cavalry, not by guns. Subsequently, Charles V was forced to take seriously the complaints of the towns against fiscal exaction and against a system of justice which served to defend the entrenched position of the landed aristocracy. The programme of reforms proposed by the rebels played a substantial part in the political reconstruction of Castile following the rebellion [50: pp. 33–6].

The reconstruction applies very strictly to Castile alone. For all its mass of territory, its American silver and its Castilian military prowess, Spain failed to integrate anything approaching a modern state. If those city-states discussed in earlier chapters declined because they were too dwarfish, the vast empire of Spain tottered because of its gigantic size [29: vol. 2, ch. 4]. The territories of Charles V and Philip II remained a clumsy *monarquia* and even the gargantuan energies of Olivares were thwarted by the particularism of Catalonia in 1640 [51].

The capital of that area, Barcelona, a city which had enjoyed considerable independence in the fifteenth century, provides an example of continuing urban autonomy. It remained largely unchanged in the age of absolutism both in terms of the space it occupied and its buildings. Its population – around 30,000 in 1516, about 40,000 two hundred years later – was sustained by a flow of immigrants clearly not distracted by Madrid. As late as 1628 the city's leading citizens were rather awkwardly described as 'knights of the city-state' and its 'archaic' civic structures – its guilds and patricians – survived into the eighteenth century. The monarchy had neither the time nor the energy to change them [71].

Naples was another scene of rebellion against Castile. The uprising of 1585 almost succeeded in creating a second Flanders for Philip II. It is well known that the leadership was divided, and fears of radicalism drove the more conservative into reacceptance of the status quo. But the status quo was re-established not by the stern discipline of a Spanish army, but by an instruction to the city's oligarchy to restore order and 'to consider themselves a republic' to do so [quoted in 72].

France

According to the titles of successive volumes of the *New Cambridge Modern History*, 'The Decline of Spain' was followed by 'The Ascendancy of France'. We miss many nuances if we assume that France succeeded where Spain had failed. The country remained little more than a congeries of regions until the administrative reforms of Napoleon. Paris itself, we should recall, had humiliated Henry III in 1588 and held out for four years against Henry IV's siege. Even the defeat of La Rochelle was not pre-ordained. In 1621, the town of Montauban had resisted a royal army and watched it strike camp in failure. Montpellier had withstood a royal siege the following year. La Rochelle itself was superbly fortified, and what is more its coastal situation invited intervention on the city's behalf [47].

Counter-factual history is a dangerous pursuit because it deals in ifs rather than realities. However, it is sometimes legitimate and judicious to ask why things were not as they might have been before establishing why they were as they were. Had Protestant British forces intervened with vigour on behalf of the besieged city, the history of both France and Britain might have been very different. The weakness of the French monarch would once again have been plain for all to see, the Protestant cause would have appeared a genuinely international movement rather than a defence of localism under the guise of religion, radical opinion in Britain would have been reassured as to the Stuart monarchy's commitment to Protestantism. In a nutshell, as Sir George Clark speculated, 'If Buckingham had relieved La Rochelle, we might never have heard of Oliver Cromwell' [34: p. 20]. In the event, the justifiable nervousness of Charles I along with his favourite's lack of vision and lack of grip were no match for the determination and single-mindedness of Louis XIII and Richelieu during the 'crucial phase' in the development of French absolutism [73].

Britain

There are observations of a different sort to be made in the case of Britain itself. The integration of the state appeared to some observers to be a question of the subordination of the provinces to London rather than to the Crown. Thomas Platter remarked in 1599 that 'London is not said to be in England, but rather England is in London' [quoted in 74: p. 155]. The expansion of the city – from 120,000 people in about 1550 to almost half a million in 1700 – depended on huge immigration which seems to have stunted other urban centres. The combined population of other towns of more than 5000 people moved from 125,000 in 1600 to about 275,000 in 1700, from only 3 per cent to less than 5.5 per cent of the population as a whole. By then London alone accounted for 10 per cent of all the people in England [75: ch. 1].

London could scarcely claim to be a city-state, for it was the seat of a monarchy which in the early seventeenth century aspired to govern by divine right. However, as late as 1617, a Venetian observer – who could be expected to know what a republic was – described the city as 'a sort of republic of wholesale merchants' [quoted in 74: p. 155]. As for the poor of the great city, relief was a question of urban experiment and initiative rather than of national policy. In hard times, the city relied upon traditional neighbourhood structures. There is more than a hint of old-style communal and civic solidarity in schemes of poor relief which involved not only alms-giving, but also the maintenance of demand to the advantage of the small trader and the shopkeeper – a mechanism and a mentality surprisingly similar to the small towns of southern Germany [76: ch. 2; below, pp. 36–40]. This is reflected in the city's culture which, with its public theatres and pageants, remained conspicuously civic despite the presence of the opulent Stuart court [74: ch. 4].

So, London's economic expansion gave it a political significance in the affairs of state and the growth of an empire [18: vol. 1, ch. 8]. But was London an exception? Certainly, but then so was everywhere else. If we could detect uniformity in the urban experience, we could scarcely make a case for the autonomy of separate urban communities. The history of early modern cities is a set of variations, but variations on the theme of scale. If we tour the urban heartland of medieval Europe, moving from London to the Netherlands, through south Germany and Switzerland, then into northern Italy, we find a surprising number of instances of city-states which expanded to compete with princely absolutisms, or which rolled themselves up like hedgehogs against external forces. We shall take some liberties with chronology, but the pattern of survival is not one which can be charted smoothly from one town to another and from one year to the next. The point to grasp is the continuing vigour of urban communities in the sixteenth and seventeenth centuries, and the ways in which their vitality influenced and enriched the political experience of Europe as a whole.

The Netherlands

Amsterdam provides an instance of survival through expansion. This great metropolis was at the economic and political centre of a world trading empire which defeated the ambitions of the greatest power on earth, the Spanish monarchy [77]. Its population, swollen by those who sought liberty of conscience, grew from around 50,000 in 1600 to over 200,000 in the eighteenth century. As Andrew Marvell sardonically pointed out in 'The Character of Holland', religious toleration and economic growth were inextricably linked:

> Hence Amsterdam, Turk – Christian – Pagan – Jew,
> Staple of sects and Mint of Schism grew:
> That Bank of Conscience where not one so strange
> Opinion but finds credit and exchange.

The problems of this vast and variegated society were imperfectly but energetically contained within a range of social institutions which were the envy of Europe [78]. It was the Amsterdam workhouse which inspired the initiatives of the Parisian authorities in the seventeenth century [31]. In 1685, James Monson, a visiting Englishman, wrote of 'the charitable inclination of the Hollanders' and 'their great care in relieving, maintaining, and educating their poor, for there are no beggars to be seen anywhere in the streets'. He commented too on the cleanliness of the hospitals, the Weeshuis, the Gasthuis and the Mannenhuis. (Despite its name this last housed over 400 poor women when he saw it.) Three years later, William Carr, the British ambassador, gave a detailed description of the system of poor boxes and asserted that Amsterdam's institutions catered for 20,000 people every day. Children were in school from the age of three, and in the middle of the seventeenth century, the Portuguese ambassador gained the impression that 'there is not a cobbler in these parts who does not add French and Latin to his own language' [quotes from 78: pp. 56, 155].

Amsterdam was not the federal capital of the United Provinces or even the provincial capital of Holland – both roles belonged to The Hague. Yet the economic power of the city – it contributed up to two-thirds of the budget of the Provinces as a whole – gave it exceptional influence in international politics, and the deliberations of the city council were of considerable moment in the world's affairs [79].

In its combination of economic power and political significance, Amsterdam recalls the great city-states of the Middle Ages. Indeed the language of politics which the city-state had provided was applied to the larger entity of the entire United Provinces. This is an important instance – which will recur – of the application of the model of the city-state to a larger territorial entity. The Dutch used the term *commune* to mean *patria*, which tallies with the way in which civitas could mean both 'city' and 'state' [11: p. 147; above, p. 1]. In a sense, then, the federation was a city-state, which was an important step, indeed a crucial imaginative leap, in overcoming the problems of scale which proved insuperable in other cases.

There can be no question that the federation was highly successful in its economic integration. Dutch agriculture had to be the most efficient in Europe to support so many urban communities – of which Amsterdam was the largest – on such a slender and unpromising strip of land. Commerce cushioned agrarian experiment with imports of large quantities of grain, much of it through Danzig, another independent city-state. Industry did not move to the countryside to clog the productive capacity of the fields [18: vol. 3, ch. 3]. Leyden produced around 160,000 pieces of cloth a year in the 1660s, yet its economy was still based on small-scale production units organised amongst guildsmen, with the guilds themselves continuing to perform important functions in society [80]: a pattern we find repeated in parts of Germany.

Germany

Here, towns of virtually no importance in the world's economy or in international politics retained their independence despite their introversion. For all the power which the princes acquired in the Reformation, a power emphasised by the terms of the Peace of Augsburg, their triumph was far from total.

In no other context, perhaps, are problems of definition

31

more pronounced. It is difficult to point to instances of full autonomy. In the German towns of the Hanseatic League only Lübeck, Hamburg and Bremen enjoyed such liberty (so did Danzig, but its location in Poland rules it out of a discussion of Germany) [81]. The 'free' cities, about seventy in all, acknowledged no higher authority except the emperor, and while they would never concede him full sovereignty, they could not dispense with his protection against the ambitions of the princes.

Moreover, it is hard to fix upon a typical size for German cities. The 25,000-strong population of Nuremberg lived in a free city, but then so did the 400 or so inhabitants of Zell am Harmesbach. A large city such as Ulm controlled a territory of some 500 square miles, an even larger one, Augsburg, virtually none [81].

Yet if generalisation is possible across this variegated landscape, it might be framed thus: neither before the Reformation, nor during it, nor in some areas in its aftermath was princely supremacy inevitable. Before religion cut across other allegiances, the cities acted in concert with the emperor against the princes. In 1492, the Swabian League, which included Nuremberg, Augsburg and Ulm, confronted Albrecht IV of Bavaria at the Lech and made him restore the freedoms of Regensburg and renounce his claims to the Tyrol. In the aftermath of the Swabian War of 1500, a margrave of Brandenburg, of all people, found Nuremberg too sturdy an opponent. The princely ecclesiastics of Cologne, Worms and Speyer found that the townspeople did not accept their authority without question. In 1504, near Regensburg, the forces of the free cities and the emperor defeated the armies of the count palatine and of Bohemia. In 1520, an alliance of Bavaria and the free cities of the Swabian League inflicted a resounding defeat on Duke Ulrich of Württemberg, ending his designs on the towns of Esslingen, Reutlingen and Rottweil. Bavaria was by no means the senior partner in the alliance, and contemporaries saw Ulrich's defeat as a victory for the liberties of towns at the expense of the princes [41: pp. 97–8].

Then Luther's call for the renewal of the spiritual life of the laity, with his emphasis on a brotherhood of Christians uncluttered with the external paraphernalia of masses, banquets, and the cult of the saints, revived the notion of the sacral civic community and pushed the cities in the direction of greater autonomy. The Reformation gave the cities a new awareness of their original communal foundations, reviving in religious form the notion of freedom through solidarity. More than 50 imperial cities recognised Protestantism, over 30 adopted and retained the new faith. Only 14 never gave official toleration to a Protestant congregation [43].

If we look at the dynamics of this situation from the viewpoint of 1520 rather than from 1555 or 1648, we gain a different picture of the threat to imperial unity which the cities posed [41]. Only two decades before, in the aftermath of the Swabian War of 1499, a number of cities asserted their independence of the Empire in the most emphatic way possible: they left it and joined the Swiss Confederation, [below, p. 42] and Basel, Mühlhausen and Rottweil later followed suit. Zürich, which had been involved in the initial secession, was the platform on which Zwingli preached that 'a Christian man is no more than a good and loyal citizen', and that 'the Christian city is nothing more than the Christian Church' [41: pp. 33–4]. It is as though he was updating Augustine as *The City-State of God*. It is clear that the Reformation had given new life and strength to the solidarity of the civic community as a religious corporation in Nuremberg, in Augsburg, in Strasbourg and in Constance. For years the cities defied the emperor and won victories over the princes. How many more of them might 'turn Swiss'? How much of Germany might they carry off with them?

In the aftermath of the defeat of Ulrich of Württemberg in 1520, the imperial adviser Maximilian von Bergen warned Charles of the Swabian League's 'strong inclination toward the Swiss', and expressed the fear that 'the whole German land would become one vast commune' [quoted in 41: pp. 110–11]. In 1525, the year of the peasant uprising (which Margrave Casimir perceived as having taken its inspiration from urban unrest), the humanist Konrad Mutianus warned the Elector Frederick of Saxony that the townsmen wanted to establish a republic such as that of the Venetians, or, intriguingly, upon the ancient Greek model. Again, it seems, the principles of the polis could guide the formation of a greater entity –

especially in the minds of those who had cause to fear such a development [41: p. 87].

The fears were not groundless. Despite the towns' virtual exclusion from the Imperial Diet after 1521, they organised their own assembly round four different geographical areas headed respectively by Augsburg, Strasbourg, Frankfurt and Nuremberg. The assembly met nine times between 1522 and 1525 [41: p. 134].

Once the emperor's stern intention to repress Lutheranism became clear, the three-cornered fight of empire, princes and cities became a religious war of Catholics against Protestants, and the towns were forced into alliance with Protestant princes. Although the cities sought Protestant friends rather than princely protection, they were hopelessly compromised, as the muddled history of the League of Schmalkalden shows.

That union of eight princes and eleven cities – including Magdeburg, Bremen, Lübeck and Strasbourg – was a sorry and perhaps unnecessary capitulation to princely power. Nuremberg advocated union with the princes but eventually refused to join. Strasbourg hesitated about 'turning Swiss', then sought an alliance with Ulm and Nuremberg. In 1528 the negotiations foundered on the new union's attitude to the Swabian League, and the moment for a powerful combination of major cities had passed. When the League of Schmalkalden was formed in 1531, its justification in resisting oppression was formulated by the lawyers of the Landgrave Philip of Hesse. In 1534, however, the League was instrumental in restoring Ulrich to the Duchy of Württemberg, his Lutheranism now as attractive as his tyranny had been repulsive.

As the negotiations of 1528 drifted further and further from urban federation, only the magistrates of Constance appeared unwilling to compromise with the princes. They acknowledged the dangers which princes and bishops posed to urban liberties:

> no longer will there be a free, German government such as our ancestors bequeathed to us, but a government of force and domination, as in other nations. [quoted in 41: p. 200]

They lamented that the cities had 'lost their freedoms and become princes' towns', and they sought to unite the cities to protect and to defend each other's land, people, liberties, rights and privileges. As the other cities' failure of nerve became increasingly apparent, the town of Constance joined Strasbourg and the major Swiss cities in the Christian Federation [41: p. 204]. Even though this alliance included Philip of Hesse, it was symptomatic of the continuing vitality of federalism. Why ultimately did schemes of union come to nothing?

As we have already suggested, both the strengths and the weaknesses of the cities were magnified by the Reformation crisis. The revival of civic solidarity was countered by the new imperial hostility which pushed some of the cities into the arms of the princes. The possibility of following the Swiss example was complicated by the growing divisions between followers of Luther and Zwingli. And there were deep historical dissimilarities between south Germany and Switzerland which compounded the other problems. The very self-containedness of the German cities made confederacy with the Swiss at best difficult. Rural seigneurialism and princely power were much weaker amongst the Swiss, and the political and economic symbiosis of towns and countryside was altogether more stable and self-assured [41; 82].

However, the history of urban liberties in Germany goes well beyond the formation of the League of Schmalkalden. Neither the defeat of the League by the emperor, nor the ecclesiastical powers wielded by secular princes after the Peace of Augsburg marked the end of urban independence. In the short term, the towns remained decisive in determining the fortunes of the League itself. Bremen held out against the imperial armies after the Protestant catastrophe at Mühlberg (1547), and this made an imperial march on Hamburg impossible. Magdeburg, a member of the League of Schmalkalden, also refused to yield. The city was promised to Maurice of Saxony literally for the taking – which proved difficult. The city's Lutheran pastors produced what was hitherto the clearest articulation of the doctrine of lawful and forceful resistance to princely oppression – which emphasises that the roots of this theory are Lutheran rather than Calvinist [12: vol. 2, pp. 207–10]. The emperor's ally, Maurice, had to be content with a victory over a relief army rather than over the city itself. And he then broke with his imperial master and allied with Margrave Hans of Küstrin, whom he had just defeated, in order to secure the release of Philip of Hesse (Maurice's father-in-law). The right to resist was now all the rage, and Maurice was set to throw off 'this bestial, intolerable and continual servitude, like that of Spain' [quoted in 42: p. 603]. We might properly ask whether Charles V would have lost his most valuable ally amongst the princes if the town of Magdeburg had fallen swiftly.

While joining the Swiss or forming an urban military alliance among themselves remained unlikely, the long-term history of Germany after 1555 can scarcely make sense without reference to traditions of urban political independence. Again, we must be careful to avoid reading back too much from too distant a historical standpoint. Whilst the towns of Germany are so often accused of obstructing the formation of a bourgeoisie capable of nationalist revolution in the age of industrialisation, it is too easily forgotten that those same towns had created and sustained the Reformation in defiance of imperial and princely power. That was a revolution in itself [41; 83–5].

The autonomy of German towns proved extraordinarily persistent, especially in the small centres of the south, with their self-sufficient economies and self-contained social structures. Augsburg was in steep decline after the age of the Fuggers, and it bordered on Württemberg, where the dukes who followed Ulrich began to build a recognisable bureaucratic state. Yet defeated Augsburg was never incorporated [86].

For once we have found a typical case, for any number of small towns seem to have retained their independence through the traumas of the Reformation and even the Thirty Years' War. In the seventeenth century, there were some 4000 of what Mack Walker has called the German 'home towns', most of them with between 750 and 10,000 inhabitants. Altogether, these towns housed a quarter of the entire German population. Thus, the history of one German in four in the seventeenth century is not that of the major territorial states, but that of Freudenstadt, Nördlingen [87], Esslingen, Braunschweig, Hildesheim, Bamberg, Eichstätt, Würzburg, Tübingen or a host of others [85]. In towns such as these, guilds and craft

36

organisations remained the basis of social and economic life. *Nahrung* – social justice, or more specifically the protection of a just standard of living through economic self-sufficiency – remained the ideal of such organisations. To this end they defended members against dependence on large-scale enterprise and kept as much of the labour force as possible in work. Whilst the small towns experienced no economic boom, they were well protected against slump.

We have already recorded the instances of Leyden and London [above, pp. 29, 31] which show that such mechanisms could function in big cities as well as small towns. At least two larger centres in Germany itself retained both their traditional patterns of social life and their political autonomy, and unlike the smaller towns, Hamburg [88] and Frankfurt [89] played an important part in the ambitions of state-builders.

Hamburg's population increased from around 20,000 in 1550 to three times that figure in the later seventeenth century. The city escaped the worst devastations of the Thirty Years War but absorbed refugees from areas disturbed by religious unrest. By 1700, Hamburg was to be compared with London and Amsterdam as a publishing centre, and the immigrants brought further expertise to textile-production and banking. Yet this was no haven of tranquillity. On the contrary, social life was fraught with tension. Hamburg had adopted the Lutheran faith in the 1520s. Though the city absorbed Catholics (from Italy, the Netherlands, Spain and Portugal) and Calvinists – 900 Huguenots arrived in the city following the Revocation of the Edict of Nantes in 1685 – it scarcely made them welcome. There were no wholesale expulsions, but equally there was no general freedom of worship: even the decrees of the Great Elector could not prevent preachers from fulminating against Calvinism. The religious conflicts were themselves criss-crossed with the agitation of Christians against the substantial Jewish community which developed from the 1580s onwards. The guilds opposed any attempt to ease the entry of members of the minority groups into the ranks of the citizens, which meant that the limited civil liberties of immigrants were never translated into political freedoms. The citizens themselves had gained a measure of

37

power from the Reformation through a system of subdeacons who controlled education and charity, but political life remained a matter of bitter factional struggles. The efforts of the citizenry to wrest power from the magistrates led to virtual civil war in the seventeenth century.

Surely such a divided society was ripe for princely picking? This seemed certain when the expulsion of Burgermeister Heinrich Neurer in 1684 led him to seek help from Celle, while the rebels in the city turned to Christian V of Denmark, thus reviving Denmark's ancient claims to sovereignty over the free city.

Königsberg had bowed to the Great Elector in 1674. Strasbourg had fallen to Louis XIV in 1681: in 1686 the stage looked set for another princely conquest. But the city on the Elbe was well fortified and absorbed the Danish bombardment. The city-state received aid from Celle, and some diplomatic support from Frederick William, but the Danish threat was repulsed without the loss of the city's liberties to another prince [81; 88].

Frankfurt was the scene of social conflicts which were still more intense. This was a smaller city, its population about 27,500 in 1700 (which even so made it larger than Munich, the capital of princely Bavaria). Again, immigration was the key to growth. The city absorbed a large number of refugees from Antwerp, and Frankfurt's half-century of commercial growth after 1580 owed much to the enterprise of these newcomers. Prosperity was interrupted by the Swedish occupation of the city in the 1630s, but outsiders still came in. Between 1631 and 1650, 2726 new citizens were registered, 68 per cent of them immigrants, and the city's importance as a centre of exchange owed much to the enterprise of Jewish bankers.

Immigrant enterprise functioned alongside the traditional economic machinery which operated to the advantage of small businesses. Retail merchants vastly outnumbered wholesalers. Guilds as such were abolished after the artisan uprising of 1612–16, but the crafts retained immense influence. The principle of *Nahrung* dominated the aims and actions of such organisations, and members continued to assume that economic independence was the key to social justice. Raw

38

materials for weavers and shoemakers were subject to group control, the butchers organised the city's meat supply in much the same way. The workshop, with its insistence on careful training and high standards of craftsmanship, remained the basic unit of production: a master craftsman rarely employed more than two journeymen and one apprentice. The ribbon-makers refused the introduction of a mechanical loom in 1662, and the city council dared not insist further, fearing another insurrection. Even new industries – tobacco processing for instance – were not factory-scale enterprises: *Nahrung* stood against such development.

> The absence of large-scale industry from within Frankfurt's walls resulted as much from the hesitation of the aristocrats to allow a large number of dependent workers in the city as from the strong opposition of the city's crafts. [89: p. 146]

Frankfurt was consumed by social antagonisms and the council could not afford to add to them. The aristocrats – a closely defined oligarchy of families, the *Geschlechter* – usually controlled some 28 of the 43 seats on the city council, and had to fight off the burghers' claims to a greater measure of influence in civic affairs. Amongst the burghers themselves, wholesalers tried to expand their businesses at the expense of retailers. These divisions were complicated further by the conflicts of the Lutheran majority with the city's few Catholics and with the larger groups of Calvinists and Jews. The latter were confined to a ghetto and enjoyed the council's grudging toleration for their fiscal utility [89: ch. 7].

Despite these sharp and sometimes violent conflicts, the city retained its political independence throughout the era of religious war and absolutism. How did this aggressive particularism survive? What made *Nahrung* viable? The example of Frankfurt strongly suggests that the persistent defence of the small man's social interests against political systems which grudged him a say, and against economic changes which might have swallowed him up, owed its continued strength to an acknowledgement that different groups had competing interests and alternative goals, to an acceptance of the reality of conflict. What made it endure in

Frankfurt – as in Nördlingen [87] and Hamburg [88], was that it made so few assumptions about social harmony as something definable, still less attainable. *Nahrung* made the city-state a viable political reality rather than an abstract ideal. In an important sense, conflict was an expression of freedom, the freedom of different interest groups in the city, the foundation of the independence of the city itself. As late as 1706, a syndic could remark to a burgher captain over a matter of imperial jurisdiction, 'What emperor? We're the emperor here, and the emperor's emperor in Vienna' [quoted in 89: p. 69].

Thus, the history of German cities in the early modern period is characterised by the retention of political autonomy despite sleepy economies in the small cities and despite serious conflict in larger communities, and the small man's species of social economy sustained its existence within political systems dominated by oligarchs. It survived the military revolution and the emergence of national markets, princes and bureaucracies, capital cities and capitalism, and remained conspicuous on the map of eighteenth- and even nineteenth-century Germany. The German towns kept alive the 'archaic' structures of the medieval commune and the tradition of urban political independence which those structures had fostered. The urban centres of Germany remained city-states in the loose, general sense in which the term is used in this study to capture the variety of political forms inspired in towns by the notion of civic independence. That said, the cities of Germany, for all their autonomy, remained part of an empire, and few could lay claim to total sovereignty. The next set of examples concerns towns which enjoyed an uncompromised and uncompromising independence.

The Swiss Confederation

The Swiss Confederation has a constitutional history of daunting complexity. How do we make sense of a political entity – or rather series of entities – which had no capital, no head of state, no common law or coinage? And how do we discuss urban liberties in isolation from the republican farmers of Uri, Schwyz, Unterwalden, Zug and Glarus, which fought off the domination of wealthy city-states such as Zürich, Bern and Basel? Indeed, how important was the urban dimension of Swiss freedom, given that the most significant of its cities, Zürich, had a population of only about 7000 in the early sixteenth century [90: pp. 107–11]?

We have to rethink our time scale too. Not only was the freedom of the Swiss rural in inspiration, it was announced early in European history. The forest cantons of Uri, Schwyz and Unterwalden had been independent since 1291 when they threw off Austrian rule, confirming their autonomy with the victory of a peasant army at Morgarten in 1315. The eight 'old cantons' were completed in the fourteenth century with the adherence of Luzern (1330), Zürich (1351), Glarus (1352) and the addition of Bern (1353). The Swiss defended their independence successfully at Sempach in 1386, despite the decision of the Swabian and Rhenish Leagues not to support their urban allies and the rural canton of Zug.

Such victories put paid to Habsburg ambitions for the time being. In the later fifteenth century, as we have seen, the new threat to the Swiss came from princely Burgundy. Charles the Bold's designs on Alsace-Lorraine and Savoy prompted the Swiss towns to take the initiative and form an alliance against him in the League of Constance. Strasbourg and Basel declared war on the duke in 1474. The Burgundian army, which had already crushed urban rebellion in the ducal homeland, was about 11,000 strong. This was barely half what the League could mobilise, and Bern alone put over 7000 troops in the field for the war of 1475–7. When Charles was defeated at Nancy in 1477, his forces were outnumbered three-to-one. The Swiss pikemen who heralded and carried through such crucial changes in the character of war and the composition of armies were the defenders of Swiss liberty, not the servants of a prince.

By the end of the fifteenth century, the Confederation was a political formation of considerable significance in European affairs. Some of the eight *alte Orten* had acquired subject territories of their own, and the Confederation itself held collective control of 'Common Bailiwicks' such as Thurgau and Aargau. Such lands had little political voice, and other

41

confederates called 'Associated Districts' (*Zugewandte Orte*) – Valais, Schaffhausen, Mühlhausen, Rottweil, Appenzell, the Grisons and the League of God's House – were sometimes liable to obey the call to war (or peace) but denied full membership.

Down to 1499, the Confederation was nominally part of the empire, a sort of collective free city. However, its members took no part in the deliberations of the Imperial Diet, and reacted sharply to the efforts of the Emperor Maximilian to squeeze revenue from them. The dispute about taxation became the Swabian War and resulted in defeats for the imperial armies at Bruderholz, Dornach, Frastenz and Calven – which ended forever any pretensions to jurisdiction which the empire retained. Strengthening their northern border, the Swiss admitted Basel to the Confederation in 1501, conquered the Valtellina and added Appenzell in 1513. The reputation of the Swiss fighting machine was enhanced by its service in the Italian wars (above, p. 14), and the Confederation profited from the dismemberment of the Duchy of Milan by extending its territory to the north Italian lakes, and gaining control over key alpine passes.

The Reformation added a religious dimension to the international military and political importance of the Swiss. The towns of the Confederation, like those of Germany, were fertile ground for ideas which preached the independence of the lay citizen and the importance of civic solidarity [91; 92]. Yet the Reformation brought about bitter divisions within the Confederation. When Zwingli was cut down by Swiss Catholics at Kappel in 1531, his body was quartered and buried in dung [90; 93: p. 413].

Zwingli's death marked Zürich's demise as the leading city of the Confederation, and thereafter the progress of the Reformation came to depend on a city which was not strictly speaking Swiss, an independent city-state very close to the pure form of Aristotle's polis [94]. Geneva was a theocratic republic, the bulwark of Calvinism – that most potently revolutionary of doctrines. Its French-speaking population of about 13,000 was not subject to France, but to a bishop, though he looked to Savoy to enforce his authority. With help from Bern and Fribourg, Geneva defeated both bishop and

42

prince in 1525–6 and held its liberty for 250 years. This was despite Savoy's subsequent efforts to conquer the city.

In 1589, war broke out again. The logic of other examples should have dictated the city's defeat. Its finances should not have withstood a princely zealot of the Catholic cause. In 1590, 88 per cent of the Republic's expenditure was devoted to defence, yet Geneva administered its way to victory. A quarter of the cost of war came from the spoils of victory, a quarter from the international Calvinist community so closely tied to the city. In sharp contrast with the Spanish Empire, we find the city-state of Geneva coordinating a war effort through prudence rather than profligacy, through the development of a limited bureaucracy rather than legions of officers, through regular payments to troops rather than the accumulation of impossible debts [95]. In its internal ordering, we should note too that Geneva was – with Nuremberg, Ypres, Lyons and Venice – in the vanguard of those communities seeking to rationalise and laicise the administration of poor relief [96].

The Swiss Confederation is unique amongst the political formations of Renaissance Europe. Its republicanism and its federalism depended on the active political participation of the citizens in communes which were more powerful than the cantons, which in turn were more powerful than the Confederation itself – a pattern of statehood which undermines the assumption that sovereignty should be centralised [82]. The Confederation was a curious enclave, paradoxically isolated and central in both political and geographic terms. However, the success of its terrain and its armies in keeping out external forces may equally have limited the possibilities of its exerting a strong influence of its own on the lands beyond the Alps.

Italy: the Contribution of Venice

What a contrast with Italy, so prosperous and accessible, so much the cultural leader of Europe, so vulnerable to political change! We have already seen republicanism overwhelmed in Florence and Siena [above, pp. 14–15]. Geographical

43

accessibility alone, however, did not of necessity ensure the extinction of republicanism or of city-states. Despite the loss of its entrepreneurs – often to Switzerland – as the Inquisition clamped down on possible heretics, and despite the 'refeudalisation' of the urban elite which became a noble oligarchy at the end of the sixteenth century, Lucca survived as an independent republic [97]. And Genoa recovered from the appalling sack of 1522 to make the Spanish Empire dance from its purse-strings. In many ways the Republic superseded Antwerp as a financial centre, and Braudel has dubbed the 70 years from 1557 to 1627 as 'the age of the Genoese' [18: vol. 3, ch. 2]. Businessmen from Genoa infiltrated every level of economic life in the Spanish Empire, particularly in Seville [98]. Ultimately, of course, the continued importance of Lucca and Genoa through economic adaptability depended heavily on the dispersal of their business talent, itself an acknowledgement of a new political matrix of empires and states in which the city-republics, the *minimi*, would be hard-pressed to compete politically.

If we seek a tale of survival, of economic adaptation and continuing political independence, we must turn to Venice, the city which brings our story to its climax [18: vol. 3, ch. 2; 99; 100]. For Venice solved complicated problems of defence, and stitched together a state under the rule of the *Dominante*. It survived defeat by the Turks at sea, and it rode out the storm raised by a formidable alliance of western powers in the Italian wars [101: chs 5, 10]. The city adds another twist to our problem by virtue of remaining both independent and Catholic – despite suffering excommunication in 1606 after asserting legal rights in clerical matters. In this crisis, the historian and propagandist Paolo Sarpi proved the worthy heir of Luther's anti-clericalism and Machiavelli's secularism, and the herald of eighteenth-century rationalism [69; 102]. Put another way, the city preserved the legacies of a medieval commune and of a renaissance republic, and handed them on to the age of enlightenment. In all these respects, the survival of Venice represents a triumph over those problems of scale which had plagued the city-state since classical times [69; 103; 104].

The triumph was not merely political, and the legacy was

more than the vapour of republican ideology. The idea that the Venetian constitution was the perfect blend of monarchy (Doge), aristocracy (Senate), and democracy (Great Council), generated a mystique around the city's system of government which became a myth. We are now much more aware that the famed stability of Venice – the city experienced no popular upheaval for half a millenium – depended less on abstract principle than on the careful regulation of material conditions by the city's economic and social institutions, a process which involved a vast proportion of the Venetian population as well as the closed caste of patricians who governed the city [74; 105].

Let us examine some of the mechanisms which preserved social stability and political independence, and try to take some measure of the scale of the Venetian state and of the problems which it faced and surmounted.

In the course of the fifteenth century, as the Turks applied increasing pressure to the nerve centres of Venetian commercial power in the eastern Mediterranean, the Republic turned westward and acquired substantial territory on the Italian mainland [106]. Vicenza, Verona and Padua were incorporated between 1404 and 1406, the Veneto, Friuli and Dalmatia between 1414 and 1423, and then the ambitious Doge Francesco Foscari pushed the state as far west as Brescia and Bergamo. These lands were almost totally lost in the aftermath of Venice's defeat at Agnadello (1509), but the state was rapidly rebuilt as the victors – the papacy, France and the empire – warred amongst themselves. Thus, in 1548, the Venetian state covered some 35,000 square kilometres, including about 2 million hectares of agricultural land. Under its jurisdiction was a total population of some 1.6 million – a sizeable entity in the Europe of the time [99: ch. 8].

The city itself, the capital of a renaissance state, remained, even in 1600, among the half-dozen largest in western Europe. For much of the sixteenth century, the city's population continued to expand within the environmental limitations of its watery location [107; 108]. Immigrants thronged to the city, filling gaps left by the bouts of pestilence which recurred throughout the Renaissance. Here is the shocking catalogue of its visitations after the Black Death: 1361, 1381–2, 1391,

45

1397, 1403, 1411, 1438, 1447, 1456, 1464, 1468, 1478, 1485, 1490, 1498, 1502, 1507, 1510, 1511, 1513, 1523, 1528 [105: p. 217]. Between 1575 and 1577, plague reduced the number of the city's inhabitants by some 30 per cent, and catastrophe on a similar scale hit the city in 1630. The city's population levels defy these disasters. The peak of 170,000 touched in 1563 was never attained again, but available figures suggest that in 1550 the number of inhabitants was about 150,000: it was roughly the same a century later, when 'decline' is supposed to have been well in train [109: p. 22].

How did the city accommodate – economically, socially, institutionally – this unstable population? How were such numbers fed? Venetian estimates put the city's consumption of grain at about 470,000 Venetian *staia* every year (nearly 30,000 tonnes) [99: ch. 8]. The machinery of supply was formidable. Venetians were habitually enraged by poor-quality bread made with rye, and by substitutes for wheat such as maize. In the later sixteenth century, the highest recorded figure for the imports of such secondary foodstuffs was nearly 263,000 *staia*, enough to feed almost 60,000 people for a year. But that was in 1587, when the amount of wheat imported was over 566,000 *staia*, nearly two-thirds of it from outside the Terraferma. That vast quantity of grain had been surpassed in 1566 (585,000 *staia*, 70 per cent from abroad), 1570 (630,000) and 1586 (572,000). Of course, there were years of dearth. In 1590, only about 340,000 *staia* came in – in a year when probably 419,000 were consumed – but for the next three years of that appalling decade, the figures for grain imports never fell below 534,000 *staia* [110].

Shortages could induce widespread misery. During the famine of 1528, the diarist Sanudo recorded his horror at the moans of the starving poor at St Mark's [quoted in 105: p. 244]. Yet Venice developed an unusually sophisticated range of social institutions to cope with such problems. The great confraternities, the *Scuole Grandi*, some of which dated back to the thirteenth century, looked after the permanently poor. They extended their charitable networks under the stimulus of Catholic reform, but they retained their own distinctive identity as Venetian institutions, and were never entirely the tools of the Counter-Reformation [105]. Whilst

46

the city of Venice made room for immigrants, the government was also alive to the problems of the subject provinces, subsidising the localities of Friuli and the Bergamasco in their efforts to combat rural poverty [31: p. 295].

The indigence of large numbers of people stands in sharp contrast to the luxuries on which the economy of the metropolis depended. Venice was an oligarchy, the exercise of power restricted a closed nobility of some 2000 adult males. There was no absolute monarch and no court in Venice, but the economy of the Republic was heavily committed to the demands of European aristocracies for expensive inessentials. These were often produced and marketed through a guild system which proved open to immigrants and enterprise, and whose social and political concerns were similar to their south German counterparts [74: chs 3, 6].

Republican Venice was no less opulent than absolutist Paris. Between 1580 and 1710, 37 new palaces were constructed along the Grand Canal [111: p. 204]. The main street from St Mark's to the Rialto was crammed with shops which overflowed with the appropriate furnishings – in the early seventeenth century Bartolomeo Bontempelli at the Chalice could refurbish a house from his own stock [74: pp. 110–11]. Even a citizen of Stuart London could scarcely believe his eyes. John Evelyn, who was later to describe the 'inexpressible luxury' of the court of Charles II, was nevertheless enchanted by what he saw in Venice in 1646. He found the Merceria 'all the way on both sides tapistred as it were with cloth of gold, rich damasks and other silks . . . to this add the perfumes, apothecaries' shops, and the innumerable cages of nightingales'. In Evelyn's opinion, the inlay of St Mark's surpassed St Peter's in Rome. He wondered at the 'strange variety of the severall nations' who traded there – and clearly few courtly entertainments could match the splendours of the Venetian opera [112].

Thus, Venice controlled a territorial state, developed a wide range of social institutions, based its economy on luxuries – and remained a republic. The cost of independence was considerable, but then so were the forces – often piratical – which threatened it [113]. It is worth pausing to consider the way in which Venice protected its independence against assault from land and sea. Whilst one can argue that its

47

continuing role as an international entrepot – a sort of renaissance Hong Kong – was of more value to Europe than its subjugation would have been, other states did not always view the Republic with such generous far-sightedness. We must remember the problems of defence with which the Venetians had to cope. In 1499 the Venetian fleet received an unexpectedly bloody nose at the battle of Zonchio [101: ch. 5]. When the Turkish menace became still more fearsome in the war of 1537–40, the government acknowledged the need to expand its reserve fleet. Given the unsuitability of much of the manpower of the mainland state, the burden of service fell heavily on guildsmen and artisans in the city itself [74: ch. 6]. In an age of soaring expenditure and of logistical problems which could ruin empires, Venice still found the resources to supply half the allied fleet of over 200 ships which smashed the Turks at Lepanto in 1571 [33: ch. 6].

The capacity to sustain a response to the changing nature of war at sea is all the more impressive when one is reminded of the Republic's capacity to recover and protect the fortunes of the mainland state. After the defeat at Agnadello by the force of the League of Cambrai in 1509, Venice seemed to be ruined as a territorial power. However, by exploiting the divisions amongst the victors, the Venetians succeeded in regaining their mainland possessions. Though never leading the way in military innovation, Venice never lagged far behind. Like most states, Venice relied on non-native soldiers. Unlike most states, Venice often had more cash than she had mercenaries. However, hired soldiers were supported by the longest-lived and most reliable of Europe's regional militia systems [114: p. 487]. In the 1570s, the close cooperation which the state engineered between government, senior officers and civilian overseers kept perhaps 33,000 troops in pay. This may not compare with the 86,000 troops in the Netherlands in the service of Spain, but the Habsburgs often recruited more efficiently than they paid, and we should recall that the army of Flanders was often jolted by the mutinies of soldiers demanding their arrears [33: ch. 5]. The compact English state is perhaps a more helpful comparison: in 1601, the army in Ireland stood at only 18,000 – and that after an exceptional recruiting drive [114: p. 487].

Apart from its troops, the Venetian state was defended by a string of sophisticated fortresses hung across its colonies. These carefully maintained fortifications formed a significant deterrent [114: p. 491], which accords with the view of the Jesuit commentator Giovanni Botero. He recognised that Lepanto was a memorable victory which produced no results, and he spotted the paradox of Venice's position 'for there has never been an empire in which mediocrity of power went with such stability and strength' [115: p. 9]. His contemporary, Traiano Boccalini – despite his views on the relative power of European states [above, p. 6] – took a similar view, though 'it seemed very strange that the Senate of that Commonwealth studied nothing more than peace, and yet with great vigilancy and assiduity did perpetually prepare for war, and that armed peace was only seen in the flourishing Venetian state' [116: p. 11].

What was the nature of the Venetian state? It was scarcely a face-to-face polis, and in some respects the sovereign power of the oligarchy functioned as a collective absolutism [69]. Yet the political structures of the mainland state cannot be characterised in terms of colonial subjection to central power, and there are hints of federalism, for there was a considerable measure of local autonomy. In Friuli a parliament retained its authority in financial and military matters after the region became part of the Venetian state [117]. Elsewhere, the excesses of local feudatories were checked by the consolidation of mainland estates by Venetian patricians – a complicated and effective process of integration rather than the abandonment of commerce by lazy rentiers [118]. As for the towns, there was a measure of executive power in the councils of Verona, guilds enjoyed some representation in Vicenza and Treviso, a merchant council wielded power in Brescia [119].

In the absence of a sovereign prince and the court that surrounded him, Venetian republicanism was preserved and underpinned by freedom from arbitrary power, by the rule of law. The principle can scarcely fail to impress, whatever the practical limitations. As Shakespeare recognised in *The Merchant of Venice*, the unbending rigour of the courts of justice was essential to commercial prosperity, and commercial prosperity preserved the city as an independent republic:

The Duke cannot deny the course of law;
For the commodity that strangers have
With us in Venice, if it be denied
Will much impeach the justice of the state,
Since that the trade and profit of the city
Consisteth of all nations.   (Act 3, Sc. 2, 11.26–31)

The sovereignty of the secular state, the autonomy of its political and cultural life, these were the republican liberties of Venice, even though the term must be understood within a framework of Renaissance oligarchy rather than modern democracy.

For, despite all the qualifications, the myth of Venice expressed some aspects of reality. It was intended to, for one of the keystones of the myth of Venice, Gasparo Contarini's *The Government and Commonwealth of Venice*, may have been written in response to the ideas of Sir Thomas More, demonstrating that the Venetian constitution was political perfection on earth [120; 121: p. 115]. Even before Contarini wrote his book, Venice – unlike the Swiss Confederation – embodied ideas which could be translated elsewhere. In 1494, Savonarola sought to establish a Great Council in his godly republic in Florence [122]. A century later, Venice was a significant inspiration to the Dutch. There was close contact between the Netherlands and Venice in the early seventeenth century, and the States General offered help during the Interdict of 1606. Domenico Molino, a friend of Doge Nicolo Contarini – that formidable opponent of papal theocracy – and part of a circle which had welcomed Giordano Bruno and Galileo to Venice, may even have mooted the possibility of military cooperation between the Venetians and the Dutch against the Habsburgs. Though this never materialised, the idea of the common interest of the two republics was expressed in the *Libertas Venetorum* of Dirk Graswinckel. This rather obscure personality is overshadowed in the history of how Venice's constitution influenced Dutch republican thought by the towering figures of Grotius and Spinoza, both of whom built their political thought on historical examples rather than on utopianism [123].

50

In 1647, the rebels in Palermo sought to introduce a republican constitution on the Venetian model [123: p. 35]. In revolutionary Britain, the removal of the king's head raised the possibility of forming a republic, and those in favour of such a change avidly sought an exemplar. Some looked in general terms to the republicanism of classical times [124]. For James Howell, and still more significantly for James Harrington, Venice provided the model: Venice 'at this day with one thousand years upon her back, Venice 'as fresh, and free from decay, or any appearance of it, as she was born' [quoted in 125: p. 54]. Venice had become purveyor of classical republicanism as it had once been purveyor of goods [85: ch. 16; 126].

Like all the city-states we have looked at, Venice was an exception. Yet more than any other example, its history reveals the essence of the city-state and the ways in which that classical form fed the political development of the modern world. Venice was exceptional in that it avoided revolution in the age of the 'general crisis'. Yet its society and its government preserved a translatable heritage of classical ideas which the Renaissance had revived, and which theorists and state-builders could neither ignore nor dispense with. It was typical at the historical level of this short investigation. For the Republic was a state centred on a metropolis which lacked the parasitic quality of a courtly capital, even though its economic structures could meet the most luxurious of aristocratic demands. Its corporate social structure recalled the cellular character of a medieval commune, yet the cells proved capable of absorbing an expanding population, training them, giving them work and charity, providing on the grand scale mechanisms paralleled in Amsterdam and London and which operated in miniature in Germany. Most important of all, Venice's political liberties and the corporate quality of social life were complementary, and established a balance between sovereign authority and freedom from arbitrary rule, a balance therefore between liberty as the sovereign will of the majority and liberty as the freedom of the individual to do as he likes – a balance which lay at the nucleus of the Aristotelian polis.

The importance of the city-state, then, is exemplified in the history of Venice, which in its very uniqueness draws together the experience of other early-modern city-states. Venice is merely the most successful of our case histories. Historically, Venice did not succumb to a prince: it was not 'defeated'. It survived to integrate a territorial state. This historical survival acted as an ideological stimulus: commentators took notice of Venice when they did not look to the Dutch or the Swiss. Yet the very survival of other republics in the Netherlands and in Switzerland, and the continuing existence of the corporate home towns of Germany had their own general significance. The early modern city-state, for all its defects as a human community, kept alive classical notions of freedom in an age otherwise dominated by a different classical heritage, a heritage drawn from the imperial age of Roman history, a heritage of princes and courts.

Conclusion: a Complicated Legacy

From one point of view, the city-state, with its charters of immunities and privileges, its oligarchs and corporations, was an integral part of the Ancien Regime, that elaborate structure of tradition which was swept away in the eighteenth century. That age saw the gradual emergence of a new social and economic context in the entire Atlantic world [127], and it witnessed the sudden and bloody emergence of the bourgeoisie in 1789 in a revolution which laid the foundations of modern democracy [128; 129].

However, the strain of using 1789 as the dawn of the modern era is beginning to tell. Some historians are less certain of the validity of such an approach and have interpreted the emergence of the modern world as a longer term process requiring a broader canvas for its depiction [67]. One of the main reasons for this uncertainty is the continuing vitality of the politics of the city-state in the age of enlightenment. 1789 in France is increasingly seen in relation to 1776 in America, and the ideological foundations of the United States are emphatically in seventeenth-century Britain, which of course experienced two revolutions [126; 130; 131]. The language of opposition used by the British in the seventeenth century must in turn be connected with classical republicanism – and therefore of course to the city-state. Students of Machiavellian theory and Venetian practice 'helped to form the classical republican tradition of early modern England and America', which links Aristotle, Machiavelli, Harrington and Jefferson in one great continuing theme [125].

But the classical tradition had in the Middle Ages acquired characteristics which would have been unfamiliar to the

Greeks and Romans. The revival of classical values in the Renaissance never escaped altogether from that medieval past as the revival of civic solidarity in the Reformation made plain. And so it was that by the seventeenth century, the classical republic was inseparable from the godly republic of the Christian centuries: the Dutch Republic was holy as well as free [77: ch. 2]. That said, we must remember that the foundations of medieval political independence were economic as well as religious: urban liberties flourished in the cities of the two great trading zones – the Mediterranean in the south and the commercial dominions of the Hansa in the north – and the chain of towns which linked them in south Germany and Switzerland. That great complex of communities serviced feudal expansion in crusade and conquest yet remained legally, economically and therefore politically distinct from the feudal world – and that is not the same as labelling those towns as 'bourgeois' societies [77; 132].

However, despite the important qualification that the social and economic matrix of the eighteenth century was quite new, that age of revolution can be linked with the revival in the Renaissance of a classical political tradition which had acquired new economic and social foundations in the Middle Ages.

This point acquires added force when we compare the experience of the urbanised West with the history of Russia, in which the role of the town was markedly different. Although the towns enjoyed considerable economic importance, they were never masters of their own political destinies. There were no laws and privileges to distinguish townsmen from peasants, no self-governing communes, no guilds. Even Novgorod, which had important commercial connections with the Hansa, was controlled by the boyars, and is not to be described as a polis. Most important of all, in Russian cities 'the number of urban slaves and semibondmen may have totaled 10 to 15 per cent of the townsmen'. Without the protection of its own law code, without political autonomy, the Russian town was subject to the state's demands for services and taxes. However, in the Middle Ages, rural areas of Muscovy lacked the manorial nexus of the West, and one must bear in mind that the Russian peasant, unlike his western counterpart, was not enserfed.

54

This was to be reversed in the period with which this study is primarily concerned, serfdom ebbing in the West in the aftermath of the Black Death, but flowing over the East with the swelling of the great manorial estates. In the seventeenth century, although the city continued in its role as a source of revenue, its lack of political autonomy meant that it offered no haven to fleeing serfs. There was nowhere to run [133: chs 1–3]. Russian towns were in no position to resist the Tsarist autocracy as the city-states in the West resisted the ambitions of princes. In an important sense, the Russian state shaped the Russian city, whereas the western city exercised a crucial formative influence on the shape of the western state.

However, one must be wary of oversimplifying the discussion, for at the heart of our subject there remains a fundamental paradox, a paradox of continuity and change. On the one hand, in theory and in practice the city-state provides one of the most powerful continuities in the history of western civilisation. 'Act', 'candidate', 'politics' are still common currency, even though they were coined in classical times [2: p. 13], and an authority on politics in the age of Caesar has remarked convincingly that 'a Roman politician would have been completely lost in the complicated organisation of an American presidential election, but he could have learned the ropes fairly easily in the type of organisation leading up to a nominating convention' [134: p. 8]. But the city-state is also one of the most dynamic sources of change. In its transformation from ancient polis to modern republic, the city-state provides in its political language and in its historical experience a capacity for innovation which never loses its feeling for the past. The history of the city-state, which this study only partially covers, is one of our most important guides to the deepest origins of the modern world.

Bibliography

General

[1] L. Mumford, *The City in History* [Harmondsworth, 1966) remains an indispensable and stimulating introduction.

[2] J. Boardman *et al.*, *The Oxford History of the Classical World* (Oxford, 1986) is a marvellous up-to-date survey, with extensive references to the polis and the civitas.

[3] M. Girouard, *Cities and People: A Social and Architectural History* (New Haven, 1985) has a rather dense text, but this is made up for by the magnificent illustrations.

[4] J. E. Vance, *This Scene of Man: The Role and Structure of the City in the Geography of Western Civilisation* (New York, 1977) gives a comprehensive typology of cities, though some of the generalisations do not convince in historical terms.

[5] G. Sjoberg, *The Pre-Industrial City: Past and Present* (New York, 1960) is an important though not uncontroversial sociological survey.

[6] P. Burke, 'The City-State, in J. Hall (ed.), *States in History* (Oxford, 1986) is a compact yet characteristically wide-ranging introduction to problems of definition.

[7] A. Toynbee (ed.), *Cities of Destiny* (London, 1967) is comprehensive and well-illustrated.

Middle Ages and Renaissance

[8] W. Ullmann, *Medieval Political Thought* (Harmondsworth, 1975).

[9] R. W. Southern, *The Making of the Middle Ages* (London, 1970): a superb introduction to the structure of society and the place of freedom within it.

[10] J. Le Goff, 'The Town as an Agent of Civilisation', in C. M. Cipolla (ed.), *The Fontana Economic History of Europe*, vol. 1 (London, 1972) is a somewhat eccentric essay, but it includes a most impressive bibliography.

[11] A. Black, *Guilds and Civil Society in European Political Thought from the Twelfth Century to the Present* (London, 1984) is a most imaginative and rewarding book, covering a vast subject with precision and clarity.

[12] Q. D. Skinner, *The Foundations of Modern Political Thought*, 2 vols

(Cambridge, 1978) is a masterly account of the emergence of the idea of liberty in the Italian Renaissance and its subsequent fortunes in the Reformation.

[13] F. Rörig, *The Medieval Town*, trans. D. Bryant (London, 1967) sets the economic and political importance of the towns in international affairs.

[14] J. J. Norwich, *A History of Venice* (Harmondsworth, 1983) is a useful narrative of the city's fortunes.

[15] G. A. Williams, *Medieval London: From Commune to Capital* (London, 1963).

[16] P. Dollinger, *The German Hansa*, trans. D. S. Ault and J. Steinberg (London, 1970) is a full and lucid account of the rise and fall of the League.

[17] H. Pirenne, *Belgian Democracy: Its Early History*, trans. J. V. Sanders (Manchester, 1915) remains an absorbing history of the liberties of the towns of Flanders.

[18] F. Braudel, *Civilisation and Capitalism (15th–18th Centuries)*, trans. S. Reynolds, 3 vols (London, 1982), vol. 1 *The Structures of Everyday Life*, vol. 2 *The Wheels of Commerce*, vol. 3 *The Perspective of the World*: a majestic survey with important material on the nature of towns (vol. 1), the character of urban economic life (vol. 2), and the role of the cities in the creation of the global economy (vol. 3).

[19] B. Pullan, *A History of Early Renaissance Italy from the Mid-Thirteenth to the Mid-Fifteenth Century* (Harmondsworth, 1973) is the most concise and comprehensive survey of the origins of the Renaissance in Italy.

[20] L. Martines, *Power and Imagination: City-States in Renaissance Italy* (New York, 1980): rather lurid, but communicates the cultural vitality of the Italian city-states.

[21] J. Burckhardt, *The Civilisation of the Renaissance in Italy*, trans. S. G. C. Middlemore (Oxford and London, 1945).

[22] R. Goldthwaite, *The Building of Renaissance Florence: A Social and Economic History* (Baltimore, 1981) is a great book which shows how the buildings must be understood in relation to the organisation of work.

[23] F. Hartt, 'Art and Freedom in Quattrocento Florence' in L. F. Sandler (ed.), *Essays in Memory of K. Leymann* (New York, 1964) is an interesting essay on the links between the city's cultural achievements and its political fortunes.

[24] H. Baron, *The Crisis of the Early Italian Renaissance: Civic Humanism and Republican Liberty in the Age of Classicism and Tyranny*, one vol. edn (Princeton, 1966): a much-criticised classic, still the starting point for an investigation of the nature of renaissance republicanism.

[25] G. Holmes, *The Florentine Enlightenment, 1400–50* (London, 1969).

Defeat

[26] H. R. Trevor-Roper, *Religion, the Reformation and Social Change* (London, 1972).

[27] T. Aston (ed.), *Crisis in Europe, 1560–1660* (London, 1965) shows some of the controversy stirred by [26: ch. 2].

[28] G. Parker and L. M. Smith (eds), *The General Crisis of the Seventeenth Century* (London, 1978) is a very up-to-date collection of essays, almost as stimulating as [21] and more effectively organised.

[29] F. Braudel, *The Mediterranean and the Mediterranean World in the Age of Philip II*, trans. S. Reynolds, 2 vols (London, 1972).

[30] R. Mols, 'Population in Europe 1500–1700' in C. M. Cipolla (ed.), *The Fontana Economic History of Europe*, vol. 2 (London, 1974).

[31] B. Pullan, 'The Roles of the State and of the Town in the European Crisis of the 1590s', in P. Clark (ed.), *The European Crisis of the 1590s* (London, 1985).

[32] J. R. Hale, *War and Society in Renaissance Europe 1450–1620* (London, 1985) is both elegant and comprehensive.

[33] G. Parker, *Spain and the Netherlands: Ten Studies* (London, 1979) is a remarkable collection of essays on the Dutch Revolt and its international significance.

[34] G. N. Clark, *War and Society in the Seventeenth Century* (Cambridge, 1958) shows how war became an institution.

[35] J. F. Guilmartin, *Gunpowder and Galleys: Changing Technology and Mediterranean Warfare at Sea in the Sixteenth Century* (Cambridge, 1974) is an important reminder of the changing scale of naval warfare.

[36] C. Duffy, *Siege Warfare: The Fortress in the Early Modern World, 1494–1660* (London, 1979) concentrates on walls and how they were breached.

[37] R. Vaughan, *Valois Burgundy* (London, 1975) condenses the author's biographies of the dukes yet retains both vigour and authority.

[38] F. L. Carsten, 'Medieval Democracy in the Brandenburg Towns and its Defeat in the Fifteenth Century', in S. L. Thrupp (ed.), *Change in Medieval Society* (New York, 1964).

[39] G. Strauss (ed.), *Pre-Reformation Germany* (London, 1972) is a very useful collection of essays.

[40] R. Scribner, 'Why was there no Reformation in Cologne?' *Bulletin of the Institute of Historical Research*, 49 (1976).

[41] T. A. Brady, *Turning Swiss: Cities and Empire, 1450–1550* (Cambridge, 1985): a superlative book introducing a complicated and neglected subject.

[42] K. Brandi, *The Emperor Charles V*, trans. C. V. Wedgwood (London, 1965): a very old book, but unsurpassed in its handling of the complexities of Germany.

[43] B. Moeller, *Imperial Cities and the Reformation*, trans. H. C. E. Midelfort and M. V. Edwards (Philadelphia, 1972): a classic study of the appeal of Protestantism to urban society.

[44] H. Holborn, *A History of Modern Germany*, vol. 1, *The Reformation* (New York, 1961).

[45] G. Parker, *The Thirty Years' War* (London, 1987): a team of expert contributors was involved in the book, but the unity is preserved by Parker's oversight and insight.

[46] O. Ranum, *Paris in the Age of Absolutism: An Essay* (New York, 1968).

59

[47] D. Parker, *La Rochelle and the French Monarchy* (London, 1980).
[48] *New Cambridge Modern History*, vol. 1, *The Renaissance, 1493–1520* (Cambridge, 1975): chapters 9 and 12 remain probably the best introduction to the character of the Italian wars.
[49] J. Hook, 'Fortifications and the End of the Sienese State', *History*, 62 (1977).
[50] S. Haliczer, *The Comuneros of Castile. The Forging of a Revolution, 1475–1521* (Madison, 1981).
[51] P. Zagorin, *Rebels and Rulers, 1500–1660*, 2 vols. (Cambridge, 1982) has useful material on the nature of the early modern state and on urban rebellion.

Integration

[52] A. G. Dickens (ed.), *The Courts of Europe: Politics, Patronage and Royalty, 1400–1800* (London, 1977) is a splendid survey.
[53] P. Burke, *The Historical Anthropology of Early Modern Italy* (Cambridge, 1987) includes a vital essay on conspicuous consumption, and much information about urban social life.
[54] M. Levey, *Painting at Court* (London, 1971).
[55] J. Brown and J. H. Elliott, *A Palace for a King: The Buen Retiro and the Court of Philip IV* (New Haven, 1980).
[56] G. Walton, *Louis XIV's Versailles* (Harmondsworth, 1986).
[57] W. Pugh, 'Social Welfare and the Edict of Nantes: Lyons and Nîmes', *French Historical Studies*, 8 (1973–4).
[58] A. Sharlin, 'Natural Decrease in Early Modern Cities: A Reconsideration', *Past and Present*, 79 (1978).
[59] D. Ringrose, 'The Impact of a New Capital City: Madrid, Toledo and New Castile, 1560–1660', *Journal of Economic History*, 33 (1973).
[60] A. L. Beier, 'Social Problems in Elizabethan London', *Journal of Interdisciplinary History*, 9 (1978).
[61] E. Chill, 'Religion and Mendicity in Seventeenth-Century France', *International Review of Social History*, 7 (1962).
[62] L. Martz, *Poverty and Welfare in Habsburg Spain: The Example of Toledo* (Cambridge, 1983).
[63] B. Pullan, 'Catholics and the Poor in Early Modern Europe', *Transactions of the Royal Historical Society*, 26 (1976).
[64] G. R. Elton, 'An Early Tudor Poor Law', *Economic History Review*, 6 (1953–4).
[65] P. Clark, 'A Crisis Contained? The Condition of English Towns in the 1590's', in the volume cited at [31].
[66] J. R. Strayer, *On the Medieval Origins of the Modern State* (Princeton, 1970).
[67] J. M. Roberts, *The Triumph of the West* (London, 1985) is an impressive interpretation of the distinctive features of western civilisation and its impact on the rest of the world.
[68] H. Lubasz (ed.), *The Development of the Modern State* (New York, 1964):

see in particular the important essays by F. Chabod, 'Was there a Renaissance State?' and E. Lousse, 'Absolutism'.

Survival

[69] D. Wooton, *Paolo Sarpi: Between Renaissance and Enlightenment* (Cambridge, 1983).

[70] E. H. Kossman, 'The Singularity of Absolutism', in R. Hatton (ed.), *Louis XIV and Absolutism* (London, 1976).

[71] J. Amelang, *Honored Citizens of Barcelona: Patrician Culture and Class Relations* (Princeton, 1986) is a brilliant study with an astute comparative conclusion.

[72] R. Villari, 'The Insurrection in Naples of 1585', in E. Cochrane (ed.), *The Late Italian Renaissance, 1525–1630* (London, 1970).

[73] A. D. Lublinskaya, *French Absolutism: The Crucial Phase, 1620–1629* (Cambridge, 1968).

[74] R. Mackenney, *Tradesmen and Traders: The World of the Guilds in Venice and Europe, c.1250–c.1650* (London, 1987).

[75] A. L. Beier and R. Finlay (eds), *London, 1500–1700: The Making of the Metropolis* (London, 1986).

[76] V. Pearl, 'Social Policy in Early Modern London' in H. Lloyd-Jones *et al.* (eds), *History and Imagination: Essays in Honour of H. R. Trevor-Roper* (London, 1981).

[77] S. Schama, *The Embarrassment of Riches: An Interpretation of Dutch Culture in the Golden Age* (London, 1987): full of insight and breaktaking in scope, this book will almost certainly prove a milestone in the writing of cultural history.

[78] C. Boxer, *The Dutch Seaborne Empire, 1600–1800* (London, 1965).

[79] J. van Dillen, 'Amsterdam's Role in Seventeenth-Century Dutch Politics and its Economic Background', in J. Bromley and E. H. Kossmann (eds), *Britain and the Netherlands*, vol. 2 (Gröningen, 1964).

[80] R. Du Plessis and M. Howell, 'Reconsidering the Early Modern Economy: The Cases of Leyden and Lille', *Past and Present*, 94 (1982).

[81] C. Friedrichs, 'The Swiss and German City-States' in R. Griffeth and C. Thomas (eds), *The City-State in Five Cultures* (Santa Barbara, 1981).

[82] B. Barber, *The Death of Communal Liberty: The History of Freedom in a Swiss Mountain Canton* (Princeton, 1974) provides much useful information, though the line between insistence and rant is not always firmly held.

[83] H. Liebel, 'The Bourgeoisie in South Western Germany, 1500–1789: A Rising Class?', *International Review of Social History*, 10 (1965).

[84] C. Friedrichs, 'Capitalism, Mobility and Class Formation in the Early Modern German City', *Past and Present*, 69 (1975).

[85] M. Walker, *German Home Towns: Community, State and General Estate, 1648–1871* (Ithaca, N.Y., 1971).

[86] J. Vann, *The Making of a State: Württemberg, 1593–1793* (Ithaca, N.Y., 1984).

[87] C. Friedrichs, *Urban Society in an Age of War: Nördlingen 1580–1720* (Princeton, 1979) is an excellent study, in some ways a microcosm of [85].

[88] J. Whaley, *Religious Toleration and Social Change in Hamburg, 1529–1819* (Cambridge, 1985).

[89] G. Soliday, *A Community in Conflict: Frankfurt Society in the Seventeenth and Early Eighteenth Centuries* (Hanover, NH, 1974).

[90] A. G. Dickens, *Reformation and Society in Sixteenth-Century Europe* (London, 1966): a lucid and manageable survey which contains particularly useful material on Switzerland.

[91] S. Ozment, *The Reformation in the Cities: The Appeal of Protestantism to Sixteenth-Century Germany and Switzerland* (New Haven, 1975).

[92] N. Birnbaum, 'The Zwinglian Reformation in Zürich', *Past and Present*, 15 (1959).

[93] G. Potter, *Zwingli* (Cambridge, 1976).

[94] E. W. Monter, *Calvin's Geneva* (New York, 1967).

[95] E. W. Monter, *Studies in Genevan Government* (Geneva, 1964).

[96] R. Kingdon, 'Social Welfare in Calvin's Geneva', *American Historical Review*, 46 (1971).

[97] M. Berengo, *Nobili e mercanti nella Lucca del Cinquecento* (Turin, 1965).

[98] R. Pike, *Enterprise and Adventure: The Genoese in Seville and the Opening of the New World* (Ithaca, NY, 1966).

[99] B. Pullan (ed.), *Crisis and Change in the Venetian Economy* (London, 1968).

[100] F. C. Lane, *Venice: A Maritime Republic* (Baltimore, 1973).

[101] J. R. Hale (ed.), *Renaissance Venice* (London, 1974).

[102] H. A. Enno van Gelder, *The Two Reformations in the Sixteenth Century: A Study of the Religious Aspects of Renaissance and Humanism* (The Hague, 1964): a difficult book, but tremendously rewarding in terms of what it says about the religious implications of the Renaissance.

[103] B. Pullan, 'The Significance of Venice', *Bulletin of the John Rylands Library of the University of Manchester*, 56 (1974).

[104] W. J. Bouwsma, *Venice and the Defence of Republican Liberty: Renaissance Values in the Age of the Counter-Reformation* (Berkeley, 1968).

[105] B. Pullan, *Rich and Poor in Renaissance Venice: The Social Institutions of a Catholic State to 1620* (Oxford, 1971): a pioneeing examination of social structure and collective attitudes.

[106] G. Cozzi and M. Knapton, *Storia della Repubblica di Venezia dalla guerra di Chioggia alla riconquista della Terraferma* (Turin, 1986).

[107] A. Zorzi, *Venice, 697–1797: City – Republic – Empire*, trans. N. Simborowski and S. MacKenzie (London, 1983) is a beautifully illustrated introductory history.

[108] G. Perocco and A. Salvadori, *Civiltà di Venezia*, 3 vols (Venice, 1977–9).

[109] R. T. Rapp, *Industry and Economic Decline in Seventeenth-Century Venice* (Cambridge, Mass., 1976).

[110] M. Aymard, *Venise, Raguse et le commerce du blé pendant la seconde moitié du xvie siècle* (Paris, 1966).

62

[111] F. Thiriet, 'Espace urbain et groupes sociaux à Venise au xviie siècle', in P. Francastel (ed.), *L'urbanisme de Paris et de l'Europe, 1600–80* (Paris, 1969).

[112] J. Evelyn, *Diary from 1641 to 1705–6*, ed. W. Bray (London, 1889): pp. 158–70 cover Evelyn's stay in Venice.

[113] A. Tenenti, *Piracy and the Decline of Venice 1580–1615*, trans. B. and J. Pullan (London, 1967).

[114] M. E. Mallett and J. R. Hale, *The Military Organisation of a Renaissance State: Venice, c.1400–1617* (Cambridge, 1984).

[115] G. Botero, *The Reason of State*, trans. D. and P. Waley, together with *The Greatness of Cities*, trans. R. Peterson (1606), (London, 1956).

[116] T. Boccalini, *I Ragguagli di Parnasso. Or, Advertisements from Parnassus*, trans. Henry, Earl of Monmouth (London, 1657).

[117] A. Tagliaferri, *Struttura e politica sociale in una comunità veneta del '500 (Udine)* (Milan, 1969).

[118] R. T. Rapp, 'Real Estate and Rational Investment in Early Modern Venice', *Journal of European Economic History*, 8 (1979).

[119] S. J. Woolf, 'The Problem of Representation in the Post-Renaissance Venetian State', in *Liber Memorialis Antonio Era. Studies Presented to the International Commission for the History of Representative Institutions*, 26 (UNESCO: Cagliari and Brussels, 1961 and 1963).

[120] G. Contarini, *The Commonwealth and Government of Venice*, trans. L. Lewkenor (1599) (facs. repr., Amsterdam, 1970).

[121] F. Gilbert, 'Religion and Politics in the Thought of Gasparo Contarini', in T. K. Rabb and J. E. Seigel (eds), *Action and Conviction in Early Modern Europe: Essays in Memory of E. H. Harbison* (Princeton, 1969).

[122] F. Gilbert, 'The Venetian Constitution in Florentine Political Thought', in N. Rubinstein (ed.), *Florentine Studies* (London, 1968).

[123] E. Haitsma Mulier, *The Myth of Venice and Dutch Republican Thought in the Seventeenth Century*, trans. G. Moran (Assen, 1980).

[124] B. Worden, 'Classical Republicanism and the Puritan revolution', in the volume cited at [76].

[125] Z. S. Fink, *The Classical Republicans: An Essay in the Recovery of a Pattern of Thought in Seventeenth-Century England* (Evanston, Ill., 1945).

[126] J. G. A. Pocock, *The Machiavellian Moment: Florentine Political Thought and the Atlantic Republican Tradition* (Princeton, 1975).

[127] J. Godechot, *France and the Atlantic Revolution of the Eighteenth Century, 1770–1799* (London, 1965).

[128] J. H. Hexter, 'The Myth of the Middle Class in Tudor England', in his collected essays, *Reappraisals in History* (London, 1961).

[129] R. R. Palmer, *The World of the French Revolution* (London, 1971).

[130] B. Bailyn, *The Ideological Origins of the American Revolution* (Cambridge, Mass., 1967).

[131] B. Bailyn, *The Origins of American Politics* (New York, 1970).

[132] P. J. Jones, 'Economia e società nell'Italia medievale: la leggenda della borghesia', in *Storia d'Italia, Annali 1: dal feudalesimo al capitalismo* (Turin, 1978) is indispensable for an understanding of the character of urban society in medieval Italy.

63

[133] M. Hamm (ed.), *The City in Russian History* (Lexington, Ky., 1976).
[134] L. R. Taylor, *Party Politics in the Age of Caesar* (Los Angeles, 1949).

Map 1   Location of towns mentioned in text

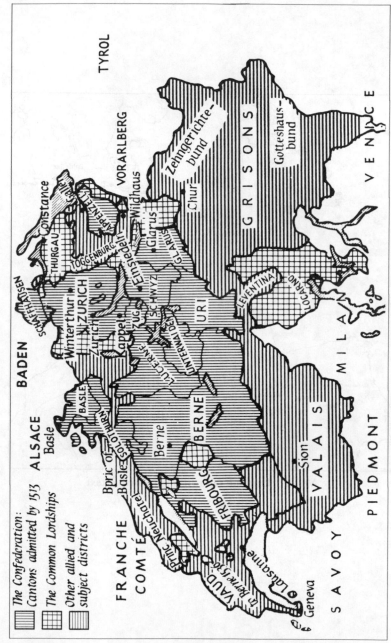

Map 2 Map of Switzerland in the sixteenth century

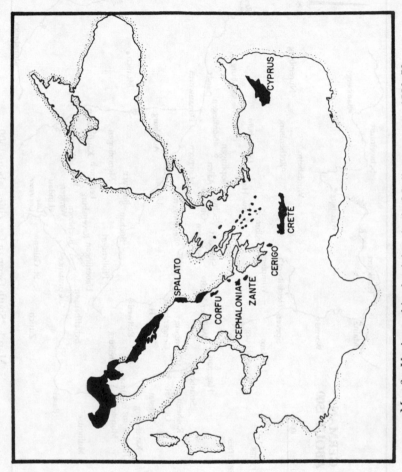

Map 3 Venice and its dominions in the Mediterranean, c. 1550–70

CYPRUS

CRETE

CERIGO

ZANTE

CEPHALONIA

CORFU

SPALATO

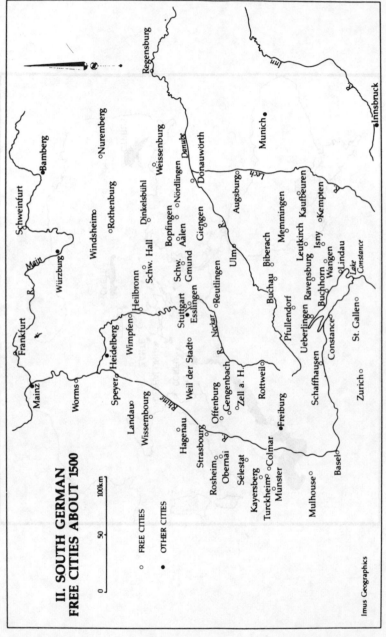

II. SOUTH GERMAN FREE CITIES ABOUT 1500

○ FREE CITIES

● OTHER CITIES

0   50   100km

Imus Geographics

Map 4   South German free cities, about 1500

Schweinfurt

Frankfurt

Mainz

Worms

Speyer

Landau

Wissembourg

Hagenau

Strasbourg

Rosheim

Kayersberg

Turckheim Colmar

Obernai

Sélestat

Munster

Mulhouse

Basel

Würzburg

R. Main

Heidelberg

Wimpfen

Heilbronn

Weil der Stadt

Stuttgart

Esslingen

R. Neckar

Offenburg

Gengenbach

Zell a. H.

Rottweil

Freiburg

Schaffhausen

Zurich

Windsheim

Rothenburg

Schw. Hall

Bopfingen

Aalen

Schw. Gmund

Reutlingen

Pfullendorf

Ueberlingen

Constance

St. Gallen

Bamberg

Nuremberg

Dinkelsbühl

Weissenburg

Nördlingen

Giengen

Ulm

Biberach

Buchau

Ravensburg

Lake Constance

Danube

Donauwörth

Augsburg

R. Lech

Memmingen

Leutkirch Kaufbeuren

Isny Kempten

Buchhorn

Wangen

Lindau

Regensburg

R. Inn

Munich

Innsbruck

68

Index

Luther, Martin, and Lutheranism, 12, 32, 34, 35, 37, 39, 44
Lyons, 6, 7, 23, 43

Machiavelli, Niccolò, 14, 44, 53
Madrid, 6, 17, 18, 19, 21, 22, 23, 27
  see also capital cities; Spain, Spaniards
Magdeburg, 12–13, 34, 35, 36
Mainz, 11
Malta, 10
Marignano, battle of, 14
  see also Italy, Italian wars
Maximilian I, Holy Roman Emperor, 10, 12, 42
Medici family, 5, 14, 18
  see also Florence, Florentines
Medina del Campo, 15, 26
mercenaries, 9, 14, 26, 48
  see also armies
Michelin, 10
Milan, 5, 14, 18, 42
'military revolution', 14, 15, 40
  see also armies; fortifications; mercenaries
Minden, 12
Montauban, 27
Montpellier, 27
Morgarten, battle of, 9, 41
Mühlberg, battle of, 12, 35
Mühlhausen, 33, 42
Munich, 38

Nahrung, 37–9
Nancy, battle of, 41
Naples, 18
Netherlands, 29, 30–1, 37, 48, 50, 52, 54
Nördlingen, 36, 40
Novgorod, 54
Nuremberg, 12, 23, 32, 33, 34, 43

oligarchy, 27, 40, 47, 50, 53
  see also patricians
Osnabrück, 12, 15
Osterburg, 11

Padua, 45
Palermo, 18, 51
Paris, 6, 13, 17, 18, 19, 22, 23, 27
  see also capital cities; France, French
patricians, 27, 45, 49
  see also oligarchy
Pavia, battle of, 14
  see also Italy, Italian wars
Philip II, King of Spain, 18, 26, 27
Philip IV, King of Spain, 18, 20
Philip of Hesse, Landgrave, 34, 35, 36
plague, 45–6
  see also Black Death; population movements
polis, 1, 6, 8, 23, 33, 42, 49, 55
  see also city-states, approaches to
population movements, 6, 11, 21, 22, 28, 32, 37, 38, 45, 47
poverty and poor relief, 2, 22, 29, 30, 38, 43, 46, 47
princes and princely power, 7, 11, 12, 15, 17, 18, 21, 23, 31, 32, 34–6, 40, 43, 49, 52, 55
  see also absolutism; courts, princely; states, formation of
Pullan, Brian, 7

Ravenna, battle of, 14
  see also Italy, Italian wars
rebellion, 10, 11, 26, 27
Reformation, 11, 13, 28, 31, 33, 35, 36, 38, 42, 54
Regensburg, 12, 32
Renaissance, 5, 14, 44, 50, 51, 54
republics and republicanism, 5, 6, 7, 15, 24, 27, 33, 43, 44, 49, 51, 53
  see also communes; freedom, forms of
resistance, theory of, 35–6
Reutlingen, 32
revolt, see rebellion
Rhenish League, 41
  see also federations and federalism
Rome, 2, 26, 47
Rottweil, 32, 33, 42
Russia, 54–5

71

72